CITIZEN DOCTOROW

Notes on Art & Politics

CITIZEN DOCTOROW

Notes on Art & Politics

The *Nation* Essays 1978-2015

By E.L. Doctorow

Edited by
RICHARD LINGEMAN

Afterword by
VICTOR NAVASKY

Nation.

© 2015 The Nation Company, L.L.C.

Published by The Nation Company, L.L.C.
Visit our website at www.thenation.com/ebooks

All rights reserved. No part of this book may be
reproduced or transmitted in any form or by any
means, electronic or mechanical, including photocopy,
recording, or any information storage retrieval system,
without permission in writing from the publisher,
except brief passages for review purposes.

First printing 2015

ISBN 978-1-940489-09-4 paperback
ISBN 978-1-940489-08-7 e-book

Book design by Omar Rubio.
Printed by BookMobile in the United States and
CPi Books Ltd in the United Kingdom.

TABLE OF CONTENTS

9	*Introduction*	Richard Lingeman
19	Living in the House of Fiction (1978)	
29	The Language of the Theater (1979)	
39	The Rise of Ronald Reagan (1980)	
51	Arts Funding for the Artist's Sake (1981)	
59	It's a Cold War World Out There, Class of '83 (1983)	
67	Shultz and PEN (1986)	
73	The State of Mind of the Union (1986)	
85	A Citizen Reads the Constitution (1987)	
115	A Gangsterdom of the Spirit (1989)	
133	An Open Letter to the President (1991)	
139	Art vs. the Uniculture (1991)	
149	The Character of Presidents: Faith, Hope and Voting (1992)	
163	Mythologizing the Bomb (1995)	

177 F. Scott Fitzgerald 1896-1996, R.I.P. (1996)

183 In the Eighth Circle of Thieves (2000)

197 Why We Are Infidels (2003)

203 The Intuitionist (2003)

209 The White Whale (2008)

225 An Interview with E.L. Doctorow
       (Christine Smallwood, 2009)

231 Reading John Leonard (2012)

239 Home (2015)

251 *Afterword*   Victor Navasky

INTRODUCTION

Richard Lingeman

From 1978 until just months before his death in July 2015, the novelist E.L. Doctorow favored *The Nation* with his comments on the American scene. Reading them now, we glimpse a literary man having his say on contemporary political and social issues.

Interestingly, in his very first article for the magazine, "Living in the House of Fiction" (April 22, 1978)—which echoes the themes of his third novel, *The Book of Daniel*, a strongly political work inspired by the Rosenberg case—Doctorow discussed the question of a writer's relationship to politics and ideology. He reached the conclusion that "ideologically committed writers" too often create works that offer views of reality framed by theories rather than by the author's personal vision.

But Doctorow realized that going too far down the road of subjectivity could lead a writer to "a sort of aesthetic solipsism," in turn leading to a genre of fiction that was all too prevalent: the psychological novel set in a private world. Too many contemporary authors had given up making "large examinations of society," he lamented, novels that were "a major and transforming act of the culture," the kind of novels that "can find out things, that can bring into being constituencies of consciousness, [that] can give courage."

In that piece, Doctorow foreshadowed much of his future work. He developed a vision that is both historic (in the tradition of Nathaniel Hawthorne, Herman Melville, John Dos Passos) and social (in the lineage of Jack London and Theodore Dreiser). Ever since *Ragtime* made a literary and commercial splash in 1975, he has given us highly original novels that slyly subvert our received ideas about the American past and offer a radical critique of contemporary culture. As the editor and critic Ted Solotaroff put it in *The Nation* in 1994: "Viewed together, his novels form a highly composed vision of American history." Former *Nation* literary editor John Leonard, writing about *Billy Bathgate*, which recounts the Alger-ish rise of an ambitious young man under the tutelage of the gangster Dutch Schultz, called it "a fairy tale about capitalism…in its first stages of primitive accumulation."

Like Doctorow's novels, his nonfiction was grounded in a set of core ideas and values—generally progressive, though not didactically so, and absolutist in their devotion to artistic and political freedom and to what he regarded as fundamental democratic principles. Reviewing one of his books in *The Nation*, Vince Passaro, a novelist of a later generation, placed Doctorow (born 1931) in a cohort affected "by their knowledge of an America their younger peers never saw, the experience of a brief period when Americanism and justice were not the antithetical concepts they later became; when progressivism had a foothold; when the labor movement became an established and significant force; when the United States achieved a kind of honorable strength in World War II." Passaro contended that underlying Doctorow's historical imagination was "a romantic love of his country, its history of democracy and violence, and its layered identity of individualism, religiosity, struggle and plenty."

In his *Nation* essays, Doctorow frequently lamented how our politics and our politicians have betrayed the nation's fundamental ideals. Take "The Rise of Ronald Reagan" (July 19, 1980), a character study of the man whose genial persona masked a corporatist ideology. "With not much more than his chuckles and shrugs and grins and little jokes," he wrote, "Mr. Reagan managed in two elections to persuade a majority of the white working/middle class to vote against their own interests." In a democracy we get the president the majority votes for. But beware of answered prayers, Doctorow observed: "The President we get is the country we get. With each new President the nation is conformed spiritually. He is the artificer of our malleable national soul."

Consider Richard Nixon, who ultimately subjected the nation to the Watergate trauma. It was indeed consequential, Doctorow wrote, that the country chose "someone so rigid, and lacking in honor or moral distinction of any kind, someone so stiff with crippling hatreds, so spiritually dysfunctional, out of touch with everything in life that is joyful and fervently beautiful and blessed, with no discernible reverence in him for human life, and certainly with never a hope of wisdom but living only by pure politics as if it were some colorless blood substitute in his veins." Not least in the power of that analysis is the final metaphor, conjuring up an image of Nixon the political zombie, his career a series of comebacks from the dead.

In a another presidential allusion ("The White Whale," July 14, 2008), he described George W. Bush's toxic cultural legacy: "The domestic political fantasy life of these past seven years finds us in an unnerving time loop of our own making—in this country, quite on its own, history seems to be running in reverse, and knowledge is not seen as a public good but as something suspect, dubious or even ungodly." Welcome to the age of the Tea Party, which would repeal the theory of evolution as well as Keynesian economics and the social philosophy of the New Deal.

But we do not read a Doctorow essay for its policy prescriptions. We read it for his firm moral vision, his glittering style and his eloquence. It's not just what he said but the witty, elegant way he said it. He brought to bear all the talents in his fictional arsenal: character analysis and storytelling power imbued with a subtle glamour. But also a deep sense of American history, culture and politics, and a philosopher's questing mind. Indeed, in another piece, "A Citizen Reads the Constitution" (February 21, 1987), he assayed the nation's foundational document as a critic would a literary text, excavating its inner meanings by close reading buttressed by references to its historical origins, the expressed intentions of its authors and its historical reception.

Admittedly, he found nothing literary about the text. It is written in the dry language of contract lawyers, sprinkled with "whereins" and "whereases." Yet behind the legalisms he discerned a central voice that claimed for itself the power to ordain. This voice is that of "the people," not God as was customary in 1787. Thus, the Constitution is a "sacred text of secular humanism," a "people's text." Its operative verb is *shall*; it addresses the future, the Republic to come—of, by and for the People. And for all its "moral self-contradictions"—most profanely, its endorsement of slavery—it immortalizes so long as the Republic lives "the idea of democratic polity."

In reading the Constitution as a "literary text," Doctorow said, he was approaching it as a "professional writer," to whom words are power. But he added that in doing so he was joining a trend among contemporary legal scholars, a trend in which he found a lesson: "When I see the other professions become as obsessively attentive to text as mine is, I suspect it is a sign that we live in an age in which the meanings of words are dissolving, in which the culture of discourse itself seems threatened. That is my view of America under Reagan today: in literary critical terms, I would describe his Administration as Deconstructionist."

Doctorow perceived a long-term, substantive trend at work that threatened to undermine the people's text: "We are evolving under Realpolitik circumstances into a national military state—with a militarized economy larger than, and growing at the expense of, a consumer economy: a militarized scientific-intellectual establishment; and a bureaucracy of secret paramilitary intelligence agencies—that becomes increasingly self-governing and unregulated." One of Doctorow's recurring themes is the sovereign role in American culture of the atomic bomb, an enduring legacy of World War II. As he wrote in "The State of Mind of the Union" (March 22, 1986), "The great golem we have made against our enemies is our culture, our bomb culture—its logic, its faith, its vision."

Doctorow's reverence for the Constitution was also evident in his essay "In the Eighth Circle of Thieves," published in 2000, in which he bemoaned the overweening influence of corporations on Washington. This corporate dominance betrays the "national ideal" articulated in the Constitution, of America as "the ultimate communal reality." For corporations do not envision a "just nation" as the Constitution does; they call for "a confederacy whose people are meant to live at the expense of one another." In such a warped polity, "the corporations…ask only one thing in return, that we recognize two forms of citizenship, common and preferred."

Prophetically, Doctorow condemned those who speak of "corporate speech" as a "kind of speech that mustn't be tampered with, as if to privilege the free speech of corporations with vast treasuries on those grounds is not undeniably to squelch the speech of others who do not have the same resources." As we now know, this view would prevail in the Supreme Court's *Citizens United* decision, which held that corporations have an inalienable right to buy or manufacture as much speech as they need to distort and influence policy issues.

In this same piece, he deplored America's treatment of citizens who speak out against "the bewildering broad front of failure and mendacity and carelessness of human life in so much of our public policy in tones any louder than muted regret." Such an outspoken dissident "will be marginalized...as a leftist, a bleeding-heart liberal or perhaps a raging populist, but in any event someone so out of the 'mainstream' as not to be taken seriously."

Ironically, Doctorow was just so marginalized after delivering a commencement address at Brandeis University, at which the then–*New Republic* editor in chief, Martin Peretz, was present. Calling the address "a calumny against America," Peretz, a trustee of the university, complained on the spot to Brandeis president Evelyn Handler. So much for a serious speech that Doctorow intended as a "critique of the Reagan administration and right-wing Republicanism." Peretz later denied playing any part in the decision not to reprint the address in a university publication, a decision that, commendably, was later reversed. In any case, *The Nation* published the speech as "A Gangsterdom of the Spirit" (October 2, 1989).

Pedants be warned: If you invited E.L. Doctorow to speak to your graduates, he was liable to tell them what he honestly thought—as he did the Class of '83 at Sarah Lawrence. "Propelled by the ethic of pragmatic selfishness," he said, "we have rushed headlong into private life and shut the door."

And he certainly did that when he spoke to readers of *The Nation*. In his *Nation* essays, we glimpse multiple Doctorows. In addition to Citizen Doctorow, the Constitution reader, there is Citizen Doctorow of the Republic of Letters, such as when he took issue with the American PEN Center's decision to invite Secretary of State George Shultz to speak at the 48th International PEN Congress in New York City in 1986, observing that artists shouldn't "need [political leaders'] imprimatur in order to get together to talk and eat and drink." Or when he defended National Endowment for the Humanities grants to writers by meshing progressive and artistic values in a democratic vision: "People everywhere have been put in the position of fighting piecemeal for this or that social program while the assault against all of them proceeds across a broad front. The truth is, if you're going to take away the lunches of schoolchildren, the pensions of miners who've contracted black lung, the storefront legal services of the poor who are otherwise stunned into insensibility by the magnitude of their troubles, you might as well get rid of poets, artists and musicians." Or when paying homage to a literary ancestor, as in his tribute to F. Scott Fitzgerald on the occasion of his centennial. Or when celebrating art as "a natural resource as critical to us and our identity and our survival as are our oil, our coal, our timber." Or when questioning the role of religion in a pluralistic society: "Our pluralism has to be a profound offense to the fundamentalist, who by definition is an absolutist intolerant of all forms of belief but his own, all stories but his own."

Just as he fiercely defended the integrity of his own work and values, Edgar Doctorow championed the *droit moral*—not only artists' *legal* right to preserve the integrity of their work but also artistic freedom as a universal *human* right. *The Nation* and the nation were lucky to have known him and to have been inspired by and given courage by his words. ∎

Living in the House of Fiction (1978)

It may be a mistake for an author to talk of his own work. It may be more of a mistake for an audience to listen to him. The author's mind is in his books—even those not yet written. The experience of the creative act does not fulfill the ego but changes its nature. As you write you are less the person you ordinarily are: the situation confers strength. An idea, an image, a scene comes to you as an act of discovery and you do not possess what you write any more than an explorer possesses the mountain he climbs. But when you speak of your own work you inevitably present yourself as an authority, and both you and your audience are deceived.

I write what I find it possible to write. I find a voice, a diction, an intonation, before I can intend to write anything. Early in my professional life I didn't know this truth and would construct outlines for books or research subjects for books—I would intend to write books. And none of them would get written. It was only when I gave myself to the act of writing, trusting it to discover what it was that I wanted to write, that I began to do work that did not entirely displease me.

It is not that you have no intellect when you write. Nor is it that you have no passions or politics. It is that nothing good can be expected from merely filling in what you already know. You must trust the act of writing to scan all the passions and convictions already in your mind; but these must defer to the fortuitousness of the work, they must be *of* it.

That is why ideologically committed writers, brilliant political persons, engaged artists, often write material that is born dead. Their ideas are stamped out on their work, cutting and forming it according to needs exterior to it. W.H. Auden said a writer's politics are more of a danger to him than his cupidity. And that's the paradox: the intent of literature is everything—its value, its justification; but the writer must allow this intent to discover itself. He must write to find out what it is he's writing or everything will be ruined.

Having said this, I want to tell you it is the standard wisdom of American writers. It is our piety. Carried to the extreme it exonerates the worst sort of aesthetic solipsism: the creative act becomes a total mystery, the artist a mystic, and any piece of pointless trash a triumph of self-expression. My point of view has turned many a writer into an academic dandy, purveyed literature as an intellectually elitist activity, and denied art any connection to life whatsoever. So like all pieties it leads directly to *sin*.

Of course the Marxist literary theoretician would condemn all of us, Doctorow no less than the dandies, for engaging in an activity, fiction, whose very form and being promotes bourgeois culture. The artist, no matter how critical or angry or politically dissenting his work may be, is inevitably a conservator of the regime; mere witness does not threaten the structure of power—indeed, giving people the illusion of their freedom in the perception of injustice will vent any truly revolutionary impulses they may have and actually reduce the likelihood of change. Even if you disagree, there is a discouraging amount of historical evidence that art doesn't change anything. As Auden said, all the anti-Fascist poems of the 1930s did nothing to stop Hitler.

In the United States there is current one literary/political movement, the new literature of the aggrieved woman, that may yet produce its magnificent work. But the feeling I have is that the women writers, no less than the men, are under direction of the culture. Rather than making the culture, we seem these days to be in it. American culture suggests an infinitely expanding universe that generously accommodates, or imprisons, us all. And one peculiar result of this is that most novels published today seem very private, or lacking in social reverberation. Everyone is talking about Private Life. It is odd, even funny, I know, to hear this complaint from a novelist. After all, what else is there?

But if you consider the possibility that human identity is changing or has changed, then it is clear we novelists don't know it yet. We have either given up entirely the large examination of society to the social scientists and the journalists, or are simply reporting, second hand, the identity they have made for us—the neurotic individual identity. Some of the writing produced under these conditions is very beautiful. But there does not seem to be any new legislation lately from the unacknowledged legislators of the world. Many seriously aspiring writers are at work, all sorts of talented writers—realists, ethnicists, fabulists, avant-gardists, genreists—and the best of us all, the most individual voices among us, seem lately only to be clearing their throats. The novel as a major and transforming act of the culture is still the desire of many of us, but for too many a receding desire. There are only two schools of literature in my country, the school that vacations on eastern Long Island, and the school that summers on Martha's Vineyard. And we have also that well-known crisis of faintheartedness from novelists who have broken and run to journalism for want of a subject.

Then what do I want? As a novelist talking about literature, I don't know what I want. A critic would know what he wanted. A novelist wants whatever it is he will write. As a working writer I can't go along with the Marxist theoretician—he may be right but the alternative he offers me is silence. I'd rather all of us, readers and writers, took our chances. Novels can find out things, they can bring into being constituencies of consciousness, they can give courage. Their possibilities are endless. But a theory is a closed system, all it can do is congratulate itself.

It occurs to me here that I might have unconsciously turned these remarks into fiction. That what I'm saying may be a story whose meaning has to be derived. After all, I first made a claim for the self-justification of fiction writing, and then attempted to dissociate myself from the conservatism inherent in the claim. I then made a vaguely leftist critique of the lack of social potency in today's fiction, and almost immediately dissociated myself from the theoretical basis of such a critique. Clearly we are dwelling here in ambiguity.

People always try to pin labels on writers or pour some sort of shrinking solution on them, and this is understandable. The problem is that we use the same language everyone uses and so would seem to express the same kind of intelligence or capacity for judgment. But while employing the common language, we give it different currency, we value it differently. What we perceive may be mythic or metaphoric but is presented in the language of factuality, and that's where the trouble lies. Writers have always been adopted by political movements and then abandoned by them because of the ambiguities latent in what they do. Fiction is a different way of knowing, it is intuitive and undifferentiated knowledge, it antedates all the specialty disciplines of a modern society, including politics. This fact is too easily obscured as artists from one age to another advance its techniques and take on the coloration of modernity.

Henry James proposes a little parable to illuminate this idea: he says that if a young woman who had lived a sheltered life walked past an army barracks and heard a fragment of soldiers' conversation coming through the window, she could, if she were a novelist, go home and write an accurate novel about army life. I find this accords with my experience. My life has not been sheltered, but I know I can hope to write well about places I've never seen and times before I was born, and about people who are not me.

Of course this is not generally viewed as a trustworthy talent. The writer sits alone in a room and composes alternative worlds, worlds that impose on, reveal, or obfuscate the real one. People would rather trust knowledge that comes to them in discreet, measurable units, identified as to discipline, and presented by experts. No aspect of modern life can be maintained now without experts. They stand between us and our experience as, for example, the medical profession stands between mothers and motherhood. The novelist, who is an expert in nothing if he is to function properly, is not a part of this system. He therefore lacks authority, which might explain why in recent years in America the writers have infiltrated the universities and established graduate degrees in fiction and poetry writing. This appalling recourse is a means, presumably, of bestowing the authority that at an earlier time we had depended on our work to give us.

The cultural role today of film directors is instructive in this context. Directors of films are society's culture heroes. Why? I think because they are artist/executives. They work in public. They marshal talent of several kinds, or experts of several sorts—actors, photographers, set designers, sound and lighting specialists—and bring them together in an intricately timed logistical process; and the result is a nonverbal, that is to say factual, material, film, that has the additional glory of having cost a great deal of money to produce. The director thus incarnates all the values of creativity, as modified by our ideals of teamwork, technological expertise and capital value. Directors don't sit alone in rooms with their language trying to figure out what is true. They hire writers to do that for them.

But I don't really see the arts competing with one another, like ball teams from different cities. Nor am I trying to place blame for the current state of fiction on life or society. That would be tedious. I'm not even sure, to tell the truth, what the current state of fiction is. Some critics I respect find the prospects hopeful. I think what I've been trying to do here is apologize for not talking more directly about my work. Perhaps the remarks will be useful nonetheless. If a person reveals himself through his dreams, perhaps a writer does so in his public statements. The condition of my working life as a novelist, as I experience it, is one of immense dissatisfaction with the form, with fiction itself, an impatience with what it has done, a terrible impatience with what I have done with it. That is almost like being in love. At the same time, of course, I imperially project from the character of my own feelings the character of our culture as a whole, and the state of it, and by necessary implication, the state of us all at this time in our lives. The insufficiency of fiction and the need to reform it, I take as metaphor for our need to transform our lives and remake ourselves. I'm sorry I feel this way but it is not from conceit. It is not a matter of thinking big but of remaining alive. If the idea of redemption itself is not by now in total disrepute then I see us all having to go at it in every way we can—politically, religiously, aesthetically, scientifically and in daily aroused perception of one another. And if the impulse comes for some wave of serene revelation, who can say how it will begin? ∎

The Language of Theater (1979)

Doctorow wrote this piece as a kind of introduction to his first play, Drinks Before Dinner, *which opened on Broadway in 1978. A book version was published by Random House.*

This play originated not in an idea or a character or a story but in a sense of heightened language, a way of talking. It was not until I had the sound of it in my ear that I thought about saying something. The language preceded the intention. It's possible that the voice the writer discovers may only be the hallucination of his own force of will; nevertheless, the process of making something up is best experienced as fortuitous, unplanned, exploratory. You write to find out what it is you're writing. Marcel Duchamp was once asked why he gave up painting. "Too much of it is filling in!" he is reported to have said. The worker in any medium had best give it up if he finds himself only filling in what has been previously declared and completed in his mind, a creative *fait accompli*. Writers live in language, and their seriousness of purpose is not compromised nor their convictions threatened if they acknowledge that the subject of any given work may be a contingency of the song.

Now, this language of the play, this way of talking, derives from two very odd sources, the prose of Gertrude Stein and Mao Tse-tung. I read a quotation of Mao's one day from a speech he gave to his officers in the field sometime in the 1930s. And the rhetoric of it was startlingly like Stein. I think now it is probable that anything transliterated from the Chinese sounds like Gertrude Stein, but I was set off nevertheless. I reasoned that a style of language common to an American expatriate avant-gardiste who lived in Paris seventy years ago and the political leader of 800 million people was worth the writer's attention.

I didn't analyze this language but merely set out to see if I could do it. It is a frankly rhetorical mode that loves repetition, the rhythm of repetition, and at its best finds the unit of sense not in the clause or the sentence but in the discursion. I have since detected a similar sound in the recorded lectures of Zen masters and in sections of the Old Testament. Once you hear it, it is all around. It's a spoken language, a flexible language with possibilities of irony and paradox that are as extended as any modernist could wish, but a simplicity to satisfy the most primitive narrative impulse. I quickly and easily wrote 4,000 or 5,000 words and took the opportunity to deliver them aloud several times in public readings in different parts of the country. I gradually understood I had composed a monologue, that someone was speaking and that he had a lot on his mind. His point of view was so singleminded in fact, and his dissatisfactions so vast, that everything he said could be answered by someone stepping a little bit to one side or the other of where he stood.

I began to respond to his remarks with the remarks of others. They were soon engaged in dialogue, and to keep things clear I had to give them all names. The one who started everything, the malcontent, I gave the name Edgar. But they were all in the same universe, these people; they were defined by how they spoke, in this heightened language that seemed to ebb and flow and rise and break on itself. The leisure for such language seemed to me to go hand in hand with privilege, Chairman Mao notwithstanding. I had a sense of time that had been bought, accomplishment of the kind our society endorses. So I put them into a dinner party (the habitual means by which privileged people wait for the next day), I put drinks in their hands, and I wrote the play.

Now, what this account says about my dramaturgy may seem to betray a serious flaw of composition. If the sound came first, the words second, and the names third, do we not have here a defective understanding of what theater is supposed to do? Apart from the fact that I find among playwrights I admire a tendency of all their characters to speak the same way, I suspect so. Especially if we are talking of the American theater, in which the presentation of the psychologized ego is so central as to be an article of faith. And that is the point. The idea of character as we normally celebrate it on the American stage is what this play seems to question. I must here confess to a disposition for a theater of language in which the contemplation of this man's fate or that woman's is illuminated by poetry or philosophical paradox or rhetoric or wit. A theater of ideas is what has always interested me, plays in which the holding of ideas or the arguing of ideas is a matter of life or death, and characters take the ideas they hold as seriously as survival. All of this is, dramatically speaking, un-American. What is clearly American is the theater of pathos wherein a story is told about this man or that woman to reveal how sad his or her life is, or how triumphant, or how he or she does not realize fulfillment as a human being, or does realize it, or is trapped in his or her own illusions, or is liberated from them, or fails to learn to communicate love, or learns, or is morally defeated by ethnic or economic circumstances, or is not defeated. Comic or melodramatic, this is the theater of domestic biography, and I contrast it to any other—classical, absurdist, metaphysical, epic—that avoids its bias of sociological realism.

This theatrical mode has been so exhausted by television and film that I'm astounded it is still thought by playwrights to be useful and interesting. Because presumptions of form tend to control presumptions of thought, even what is most basic—the solicitation of emotion from an audience—must be questioned if the emotion is no more, finally, than self-congratulatory. Having written this play and seen it through its first production, I understand Brecht's disavowal of standard theatrical emotion not only as an ideological decision but as a felt abhorrence for what is so cheaply and easily generated. Since the onslaught of television in the late 1940s, the dramatic mode has swept through all the media; everything is dramatized—news events, the weather, hamburgers. The responsiveness of the media, print or electronic, to every new idea or event or terror is so instantaneous that, as many people have pointed out, experience itself has lost its value, which is to say life as an experience rather than as a postulate for dramatic statement has begun to disappear from our understanding.

Every protest, rage, every critique, is absorbed by our dramatizing machinery and then reissued in appropriate form. The writer confronts not only moral hideousness but the globally efficient self-examination in dramatic terms of that hideousness. Where is wisdom? Everyone has faster hands than the artist. His devices and tricks of the trade have long since been appropriated not only by the media but by the disciplines of social science, whose case studies, personality typing and composite social portraiture are the industrialized forms of storytelling.

What are the presumptions of thought determined by the formal presumptions of this play? As it happens, the corruption of human identity is exactly the preoccupation of the speaker or character (not to be coy) who sets off the action, and whose point of view annoys, frightens and, if I'm right, finally enlightens the others. This is Edgar, whose complaint is with the weak Self that loses its corporeality to the customs and conventions and institutions of modern life. His dissatisfaction is so immense that he pulls a gun and looks for someone to blame.

But not only Edgar but all of the others too who join him in dispute speak in terms of human numbers, in images of replicating humanity, and of themselves not as individuals but as members of larger classes, and for a good deal of the time, but especially at the beginning of the play, their argument is in the first- and third-person plural. And when Edgar pulls the gun it turns out that he is crucially unattached to the act: it is the situation that determines what he is doing, the others define him as much as he defines himself, and his own intentions are something he may learn only as they occur—not before. The images of replicating humans are reflected onstage in this one person divided from his subconscious impulses.

So my characters are formal expressions of the basic passion of the play—an imitative fallacy perhaps, but only if you want from the theater what you're used to. They seem to be uniformly well-to-do and reasonably well educated, but they have no domestic biographies to offer, no childhoods to remember, no religion, no regional identification. Deprived of virtually everything else, they can only have their being from their positions in the dialogue.

Drinks Before Dinner deals in general statements about the most common circumstances of our lives, the numbers of us, the cars we drive, the television we watch, the cities we live in, our contraception and our armaments, and our underlying sense of apocalypse. None of these circumstances are visible onstage except as imagery makes them visible. Instead of a play in which specific biographies suffer experience that we enlarge upon to reflect our own, instead of a progression from the particular person to the thematic implication, we have a play already in the region of the implicatory when the curtain rises. That is why it is so offensive. It is a play turned inside out. It displays human beings not filled in with the colors and textures of their individual peculiarity but delineated from the outlines provided by the things that shape them, their technology, their failing rituals and faltering institutions, their platitudinous ideas and common fears. They are invisible presences, these people, ghosts, shown only as a space in their surroundings. Like Wells's Invisible Man, they can be seen only when wrapped in bandages.

Since the character of Edgar carries the burden of the argument, he is the center of the play's offense. Edgar is insufferable. He insists upon talking about what everyone knows. He is not a criminal psychopath, nor is he a revolutionary—two suggestions the others come up with to explain his behavior. He is not a psychopath, because he is fully connected to the realities of his life and is more interested, I suspect, in dramatizing the issues that obsess him, or in sharing his passion, than in killing or taking revenge. (The culmination of his violence occurs only when Alan, a man of power, seems unwilling to accept the moral responsibilities of his office.) And he is not a radical, because he offers no analysis as to why things are as he finds them. He can feel, he can describe, but he cannot explain. What he is, truly, is a person suffering from acute moral revulsion, he is a moral hysteric who has reached the limits of his endurance.

In fact, he sports some of the more unfortunate characteristics of the ancient prophets. Prophets went about exaggerating everything that was wrong in their society and they warned what would happen if things didn't change. They made dramatic, symbolic gestures to get their ideas across to people who didn't want to hear them: Isaiah went out naked and Jeremiah wore a yoke around his neck. Edgar brandishes a gun, the device of a world perfecting itself for Armageddon, but as with his antecedents, to make people listen whether they would like to or not. Certainly it is an arrogant role to choose for oneself, and for his trouble Edgar suffers the expropriation of his faith in the idea of the end of the world—the theological hope of redemption, of the possibility of something more through suffering and universal purgation. So the joke is on him. Nevertheless, a community of perception has been formed. Condemned, renounced and alone—dinner about to be served. ∎

The Rise of Ronald Reagan (1980)

Ronald Reagan was born in 1911 in rural Illinois. His father, John Edward Reagan, was a store clerk and erstwhile merchant whose jobs took the family to such towns as Galesburg, Monmouth and Dixon—just the sorts of places responsible for one of the raging themes of American literature, the soul-murdering complacency of our provinces, without which the careers of Edwin Arlington Robinson, Sherwood Anderson, Sinclair Lewis and Willa Cather, to name just a few, would never have found glory. The best and brightest fled all our Galesburgs and Dixons, if they could, but the candidate was not among them.

The Reagans were a poor, close, hard-working family.

With his older brother, Neil, Reagan sold homemade popcorn at high school football games and was charged with the serious business of maintaining the family vegetable garden. For many summers he worked as a lifeguard at Lowell Park on the Rock River in Dixon, pulling seventy-seven people out of the water by his own count and socking away most of his salary to make up college tuition.

The candidate attended Eureka College in Eureka, Illinois. He was no student. He had a photographic memory, and it was this trait, rather than application to books or innate cleverness, that got him through his exams. What really interested him was making the football team, pledging a fraternity, debating and acting in campus theatricals. But his priorities were correct. Eureka, a fifth-rate college, provided meager academic credentials to its graduates. But a third-rate student at a fifth-rate college could learn from the stage, the debating platform, the gridiron and the fraternity party the styles of manliness and verbal sincerity that would stand him in good stead when the time came to make his mark in the world. In fact, the easy, garrulous charm Reagan developed at Eureka got results very quickly. Graduating in the depths of the Depression, he had no trouble finding a job as a radio announcer.

We have these facts from a biography, *The Rise of Ronald Reagan*, by Bill Boyarsky, a California journalist, and from the candidate's autobiography, *Where's the Rest of Me?*, the title of which is taken from his most memorable line as a film actor. In the picture *King's Row*, he played the role of a young rake who is careless with his attentions to the daughter of a surgeon; when he lands in the hospital after a car accident, the vengeful surgeon amputates his legs. Reagan delivers the memorable line coming to after the operation.

It was when he became a sportscaster for WHO in Des Moines that Reagan's peculiar affinity for simulated life began to emerge. He was called on to describe baseball games played by the Chicago White Sox and the Cubs on the basis of Western Union messages telegraphed from the ballpark. These were characteristically brief—a hit, a walk and so on—but the chatty Reagan made an art of describing the game as if he were sitting in the stands, faking the scene in all its drama with only a sound effects man to help him. He became quite popular with the regional audience and did promotional work on the side as the station's celebrity speaker, giving talks to fraternal lodges, boys' clubs and the like, telling sports stories and deriving from them Y.M.C.A. sorts of morals.

In 1937, Reagan went to Santa Catalina Island to cover the Chicago Cubs in spring training. The proximity to Hollywood revived his collegiate ambition to act, and he managed to get himself a screen test. He didn't really expect anything to come of it but was offered a contract by Warner Brothers for $200 a week. An agent had persuaded the studio that he was another Robert Taylor. Considering that actor's negligible store of animation, one can wonder now at the inducement. In any event, the candidate acted in more than twenty "B" pictures before his big break came. In 1940, he persuaded Jack Warner to give him the role of George Gipp, the doomed Notre Dame football hero, in *Knute Rockne, All American*, a film about the famous football coach. His means of persuasion was a photograph of himself in his Eureka College jersey and helmet.

Subsequently, he was sanctified to play the role of a pubescent Shirley Temple's first screen beau in *That Hagen Girl*. There is no evidence that between takes they exchanged Republican philosophies. Thereafter his career ascended to such heights as the aforementioned *King's Row*, *The Voice of the Turtle* and *The Hasty Heart*; descended to the likes of *Bedtime for Bonzo*, in which the lead was a chimpanzee, and sank forever in *Hellcats of the Navy*, a black and white 1950s film about submarines. All in all, Reagan acted in close to fifty movies over a twenty-year period and the relevance of this achievement to a presidential candidacy should not go unexamined.

With few exceptions, film stars in the 1930s and 1940s lived in a peculiar state of public celebrity and private humiliation. It was the primary condition of their fame that their worth was constantly under question. The studios had a lock on everyone, and actors were punished and rewarded and otherwise dealt with as children by the paternalistic film moguls who held their contracts. Stars were property. In most cases their personal lives were as closely directed as their film lives. How and with whom they conducted themselves were the responsibilities of publicity departments. Their names were changed, and plastic surgeons improved their faces. All in all, they lived in that meld of life and art typecasting we call stardom but which is in fact self-obliteration.

Films were made then, as they are today, not by actors but by producers, directors and technicians. The working life of a star was tedium—waiting for the technicians to get around to them, doing scenes in no reasonable order, more often than not repeating them to the point of distraction. No sane adult could long take pride in this sort of mannequin work. Actors bloomed and faded, destroyed themselves in scandal, drugs and drink, gave themselves to public rebellion, or cultivated a rampant narcissism. A few even tried to produce and direct their own films. It is instructive that Ronald Reagan resorted to none of these stratagems of protest and self-expression. He seemed to agree with assessments of his talents as modest. He did not burningly aspire to serious acting. He followed the rules of the game, was easygoing and cooperative, made friends of influential gossip columnists and producers, sought contacts and acted generally the good boy, perceiving through the endless reaches of this devastatingly hollow life one salient fact: it was a good living. Perhaps if his talent had been greater or his need to accomplish something really worthwhile had been stronger, he wouldn't have lasted as long as he did.

At the beginning of World War II, Reagan, a reserve second lieutenant in the cavalry, was called up for active duty. Here, presumably, was the occasion for reality to make its intrusive claims on the life of a professional fantasist. But he was assigned to the First Motion Picture Unit of the Army Air Corps and spent the war at the Hal Roach studio in Culver City. He narrated training films, one of the most notable being *Target Tokyo*. Saipan-based B-29 superfortress pilots preparing to firebomb Japanese war plants in Ota were shown—by means of special effects, miniature topography and traveling shots made from a moving crane—how the ground below would appear as they made their bombing run.

Only after the war did Reagan's life begin to attach to the nonfictive structure of things. He became active in the Screen Actors Guild and after a time was elected its president. Of course it was not exactly a blue-collar union that had on its rolls Gary Cooper, Spencer Tracy, future Republican Senator George Murphy and Republican presidential TV adviser Robert Montgomery. Nevertheless, this was the postwar period of tough jurisdictional disputes between movie craft unions, one reputedly led by gangsters, and it was also the time when the House Un-American Activities Committee began to ask movie stars their opinions of the international godless Communist conspiracy. The candidate got a behind-the-scenes view of some rough politics. He seemed to like it well enough, testifying before the HUAC subcommittee and taking a militantly square-jawed stand on these matters of national urgency with the same kind of Midwestern good-boy appeal that was later to attract the attention of some conservative Californians looking around for a gubernatorial candidate in the 1960s.

The odd thing, though, was that while Reagan was devoting more and more time to being spokesman for the Screen Actors Guild, his career as an actor was going into decline. Paradoxically, he was getting more press and prestige as a union officer than as an actor. It is generally believed that this period of his life marked the transition from actor to politician. But in effect he was becoming an actor figure, a front for working actors, and though his activities were now clearly in the realm of the real, if insane, world, the personal quotient of pretense was still high. He was a union official pretending to be a successful movie star.

It was in this Pirandelloesque state of being that he married a fairly obscure M-G-M contract player named Nancy Davis. The circumstances that brought them together are worth noting. The daughter of an ultraconservative Chicago surgeon, Miss Davis became concerned when she began to receive mail from left-wing organizations in the early 1950s. She consulted the director Mervyn LeRoy, who suggested that they bring the problem to the attention of guild president Reagan. This seemed to Miss Davis a splendid idea—apparently she was happy to have any pretext to meet the handsome actor. The director phoned Reagan, who consulted union membership files, found that Miss Davis's name had been confused with that of another actress and gave her a clean bill of health. LeRoy, unlikely cupid though he was, suggested that Reagan bring the good news personally to Miss Davis by taking her out to dinner. Reagan complied, and it was in this manner, after giving her a loyalty check, that Ronald Reagan met his wife-to-be.

The final formative period in the candidate's history of self-realization is the eight years or so he spent as the face and voice of the General Electric Company, selling its products and benign motives to the American public on television. He introduced the weekly stories of the G.E. Theater and gave the sales pitch. But that wasn't all. When he was not on camera he went around to the G.E. plants, shaking hands with the assembly-line workers and giving speeches at middle-management luncheons. The chief executives of G.E. were at this time concerned about employee morale—not job security or better pay—but a smile and a handshake from a movie star was their formula for improving it. In truth, it was this period and not his tenure as a union official that manifested the political content of the candidate's life and passion. He began to perfect a speech, the same speech he gives to this day with ever-changing topical references and gags to keep it fresh, in which all the nostalgia for his Midwestern boyhood—the ideals of self-reliance, hard work, belief in God, family and flag—came into symbolic focus in the corporate logo hanging like a knight's coat of arms behind the dais.

Peculiarly, his tenure as G.E. spokesman overlapped the years in which the great electrical industry price-fixing scandal was going on. While Reagan extolled the virtues of free enterprise in front of the logo, G.E., along with Westinghouse, Allis-Chalmers and other giant corporations, was habitually controlling the market by clandestine price fixing and bid rigging agreements, all of which led, in 1960, to grand jury indictments, in what was characterized by the Justice Department as the largest criminal case ever brought under the Sherman Anti-Trust Act. Three G.E. executives pleaded guilty and went to jail. The company was fined, and some people to this day think Ralph Cordiner, the chairman of the board, himself narrowly escaped prosecution. Reagan, of course, was totally innocent of all of this; and there is no indication his innocence was ever shaken by the news.

Even now, as the Republican candidate for the presidency, he would probably be shocked if it were suggested to him that today the Horatio Alger hero is a multinational corporation. William Safire quotes him as saying that he doesn't want to use the word "ideology" in his speeches because the American people think it's a "scare word." More likely he doesn't think he should be unfairly tagged with having one. The pictures of him in the newspapers as often as not show him in his prewar pompadour, smiling somewhat quizzically at age 69, as if not quite understanding why others don't perceive the rational, logical, inevitable, but above all descriptive American truth of his politics.

Those journalists who have studied his years as Governor of California find Reagan's record was not all that bad—surprisingly moderate in many areas, and certainly within the normal range of the politics of compromise, the giving and taking between executive and legislative branches that keeps most governments of this country, state as well as federal, in centrist balance. That may be encouraging to some, but of all his previous job experiences, as sportscaster of invisible ball games, studio actor, Culver City commando, television salesman, the governorship of California probably has least relevance to his presidential candidacy. His own accounts of what he did in California are charmingly demagogic, as though he is seeking to prove that he was more conservative in office than he is given credit for. Some reports have it that he did not act like a Governor, that he went home at five o'clock in the afternoon and forgot the job until the next morning. He scrupulously kept his private life private—very odd in the American political tradition, where one's spouse, children, parents, sisters and brothers, medical problems and psychological difficulties are all grist for the mill. The impression is that he turned his Governor's persona on and off with a ventriloquial indifference.

The candidate has chosen not to travel abroad in the only available time before the campaign begins in earnest, because he doesn't want to give his opponents the chance to accuse him of trying to acquire instant expertise in his weak department, foreign policy. Always image-conscious, he has not thought, nor, apparently, have his advisers, that by going abroad he might possibly learn something.

In any event, the nomination is his who has pursued it giving pep talks and doing dinners and shaking hands and smiling and raising money and speaking simplistic fantasy for most of his adult life. One could write of the people behind Ronald Reagan, but that is another story. He has beaten the best the Republican primaries have had to offer—Senators and Governors, Cabinet officials, Congressmen—and the party that honored us with Richard Nixon will now offer him. Ladies and Gentlemen, I give you the next President of the United States. ∎

Arts Funding for the Artist's Sake (1981)

A statement to the House Interior Appropriations Subcomittee of the House Appropriations Committee on drastic cuts in federal funding for the arts.

I have always disliked the phrase "the arts." It connotes to me furs and black ties and cocktail receptions, the patronage by the wealthy of work that is tangential to their lives, or that fills them not with dread or awe or visionary joy but with self-satisfaction.

"The arts" have nothing to do with the loneliness of writers or painters working in their rooms year after year, or with actors putting together plays in lofts, or with dancers tearing up their bodies to make spatial descriptions of the hope of beauty or transcendent truth.

So as a working writer I distinguish myself from the arts community. I am confirmed in this when I look at the National Endowment for the Arts board and program structure. In the past a very small percentage of the arts budget has been given over to literature, to the grants made to young writers or dramatists or poets of promise. In all the time since its founding the N.E.A. has found only four writers worthy to sit on its immense board. Instead, the heavy emphasis has been on museums, opera companies, symphony orchestras: just those entities that happen to cater to patrons of "the arts."

I suppose I would have to confess, if asked, that I feel about opera, for instance, that it is not a living art in this country, that we do not naturally write and produce operas from ourselves as a matter of course as, for example, Italy did in the nineteenth century, and that, therefore, as wonderful and exciting as opera production may be, it is essentially the work of conservation of European culture; opera companies are conservators of the past, like museums, and their support by the National Endowment reflects the strong bias or belief in the arts as something from the past rather than the present.

The National Endowment programs I value most are just those likely to be proscribed: first, the programs of individual grants to individual artists in whatever medium—

the programs endowing directly the work of living artists; and, second, those programs that do not separate the arts from life, from our own life and times but emphasize the connection—the artists-in-education program, the poets who go into schools, for example, and help children to light the spark in themselves. I cannot imagine anything more responsible than the work of persuading a schoolchild to express his or her anguished or joyful observations—and to be self-rewarded with a poem or a painting. Whole lives ride on moments like that.

Or the *inter-arts* programs, the *folk arts*, the *expansion arts*—*all* bureaucratic terms for encouraging experiment and risk-taking on the part of artists, and for bringing artists in contact with people everywhere in the country, connecting people with the impulses in themselves. Programs that encourage participation rather than the passive receipt of official art of the past are the ones I think most important: all the programs which suggest to people that they have their own voices, that they can sing and write of their own past—people in their churches, students in their classes, or prisoners in their cells. These programs—just the ones branded so vilely in the Heritage Foundation Report as instruments of social policy or public therapy, and slated for extinction by our new budgeteers—are the ones I value. And not from any vague idealistic sentiment either: I know as an artist where art comes from. I know there is a groundsong from which every writer lifts his voice, that literature comes out of a common chorus and that our recognition of the genius of a writer—Mark Twain, for example—cannot exclude the people he speaks for.

Art will arise where it is least expected and usually not wanted. You can't generate it with gala entertainments and $200-a-plate dinners. You can, if you're an enlightened legislative body, see to it that you don't ipso facto create an official state art by concentrating your funding on arts establishments. Other people may talk of how many billions of dollars of business is produced from the arts, but to me that is beside the point. I tell you that an enlightened national endowment first of all puts its money on largely unknown obsessive individuals who have sacrificed all the ordinary comforts and consolations of life in order to do their work. And it sees to it, second of all, that these individuals are brought into contact with their communities. That's *my* idea of a national endowment: a National Endowment for Artists.

A museum, an opera company, or a symphony orchestra, after all, has access to private funding—some of the arts are the natural taste of the privileged among us. But a community that puts on its own play by its own unknown playwright, or brings in a poet to teach a writing class at a public library, has no source of funding other than the tax revenues to which it has contributed.

But saying even this, I cannot avoid the feeling that it is senseless for me to testify here today. People everywhere have been put in the position of fighting piecemeal for this or that social program while the assault against all of them proceeds across a broad front. The truth is, if you're going to take away the lunches of schoolchildren, the pensions of miners who've contracted black lung, the storefront legal services of the poor who are otherwise stunned into insensibility by the magnitude of their troubles, you might as well get rid of poets, artists and musicians. If you're planning to scrap medical care for the indigent, scholarships for students, daycare centers for the children of working mothers, transportation for the elderly and handicapped—if you're going to eliminate people's public service training jobs and then reduce their unemployment benefits after you've put them on the unemployment rolls, taking away their food stamps in the bargain, then I say the loss of a few poems or arias cannot matter. If you're going to close down the mental therapy centers for the veterans of Vietnam, what does it matter if our theaters go dark or our libraries close their doors?

The character of this new Administration reminds me of nothing so much as some evil landlord from a melodrama, one of those old-time landlords with a black silk hat and a waxed mustache rubbing his hands and chortling with glee as he slips into Washington. I am waiting for a rising sound of protest from the halls of Congress, but I have not yet heard declared what we all know to be true—that the so-called economic policy issuing from this government, for all its supply-side jargon and budgetary pieties, is a simple, undeniable eviction procedure, a brutal eviction of not only widows and children but all citizens except the already privileged, all interests except those of wealth and business. As a writer of fiction I could not get away with a portrayal of such unmitigated and sanctimonious cruelty; no landlord this infamous would be believed in a fiction of mine. Yet here he is, in one of his guises, pointing to charts and budget ledgers telling us who lives and who dies, and here he is in another, testifying about all the bombs and missiles we'll be able to make from the money we take away from the poor.

And so in my testimony for this small social program I am aware of the larger picture and, really, it stuns me. What I see in this picture is a kind of sovietizing of American life, guns before butter, the plating of this nation with armaments, the sacrifice of everything in our search for ultimate security. We shall become an immense armory. But inside this armory there will be nothing, not a people but an emptiness; we shall be an armory around nothingness, and our true strength and security and the envy of the world—the passion and independent striving of a busy working and dreaming population committed to fair play and the struggle for some sort of real justice and community—will be no more. If this happens, maybe in the vast repository of bombs, deep in the subterranean chambers of our missile fields, someone in that cavernous silence will remember a poem and recite it. Maybe some young soldier will hum a tune, maybe another will be able to speak the language well enough to tell a story, maybe two people will get up and dance to the rhythm of the doomsday clock ticking us all to extinction. ∎

It's a Cold War World Out There, Class of '83 (1983)

My dear graduating seniors: As Sarah Lawrence students you've avoided a lot of the traditional collegiate things, but you cannot avoid the commencement address. I represent your faculty's last shot at you, their last chance to tell you what they meant—before you slip out of their grasp forever.

Actually, they're stunned to see you here, shining and beautiful in your orderly rows a mere four years after you arrived as an unruly lot of half-educated roughnecks. So this day is a victory for them—that they have impressed on you, to the point of graduation, the model of their scholarship, their passion of intellect.

It's a victory too for your parents sitting off to the side there, weak and gasping, having had to pay for the whole thing. And, in truth, this day is a victory for you—a victory over sloth, procrastination, panic; over sleep, beer, dope, unrequited love, requited love and video games.

You may not be aware of what your education has consisted. You are aware of the courses of study, the papers, the reading. You are perhaps aware of academic disciplines as eternal, unchanging structures, public monuments to be climbed, walked around, photographed and *done.*

In fact, everything you have learned is a quite volatile composition made up by others just like you and therefore subject to your additions and corrections. What has been going on, really, is the life of your own mind as it has found the words, the ideas, the feelings to illuminate itself.

And if members of this faculty have seemed to you at various times to possess commanding intellectual presence, and I hope they have, the truth is they are itinerants, like you, having given their lives over to the strange species-grooming that is peculiarly Homo sapient—the modest, exhausted instruction in mind-survival of the generation that will succeed theirs.

And everything impractical they've given you—lines of poetry, phrases of music, philosophical propositions, ancient histories, myths, dance steps—is terribly practical; is, in fact, the only means we have to defend the borders of a magnanimous, humanist civilization.

Right now that civilization is under considerable attack. It has been under siege since 1945. You are not old enough to remember when there was no Bomb; I am barely old enough to remember, myself. But it is a most unprecedented condition for living. More and more we are showing signs of becoming unnerved by it.

As a writer, I can tell you of my personal experience in dealing with it. Inside the novelist's mind the nuclear weapon loses its political and military character entirely. What is unsettling about the writing of fiction now is that the story of any individual, and I don't care who it is, may not be able to sustain an implication for the collective fate. If that is so, it is a serious setback to people in my trade. There is a loss of consequence, and the very assumption that makes fiction possible, the moral immensity of the single soul, is under derisive question because of the Bomb.

I don't mean to imply that the problems of writers aren't the least of our problems, but only that in all sorts of ways, even as it sits there quietly in its silos, it is going off.

At least one segment of the American intellectual community has entirely lost its nerve. Its members are called, politely enough, neoconservatives, but their shrill judgments of contemporary literature are not so much conservatism as babbittry. They feel we writers aren't saying enough that is positive about America; in fact, that our raison d'être as artists is the undermining of the very system that supports us. I am not exaggerating. There is a strong presumption among them that our social critiques are not acts of love but acts of treason. I cannot believe that a previously estimable group of intellects would have fallen so sadly into ruin had the rigors of cold war ideology not broken them.

Our psychic deterioration goes beyond intellectual life. In the past ten years there has been a terrible loss of moral energy in art, in politics, in social expectations. Propelled by the ethic of pragmatic selfishness, we have rushed headlong into private life and shut the door. In the name of rugged individualism, we celebrate greed, gluttony and social coercion. And real individualism, by contrast, is a commitment to a very tough, embattled life. In this society there is an awful heavy weight of conforming behavior. The great electoral contests of our time are between the far right and the moderately right. We run for our revelation in ever-increasing numbers along the streets, on the highways. And in our fear we have elected the most foolish and insufficient President in our history, the fervent simplicities of whose mind are like a gigantic billboard advertising our ruin.

But he is ours, and we are his. Let me illustrate: last year, within days of the massacre of some 600 Palestinian refugees in West Beirut by Christian Phalangist allies of Israel, 350,000 Israelis, nearly one-tenth of the country's population, rallied in Tel Aviv to demand the resignation of their Prime Minister and Minister of Defense. Under the aegis of the United States and with American money and weapons, equally hideous massacres of the Salvadoran peasantry by the government of that country have caused only sporadic protest in the United States. Nobody has even thought of demanding the resignation of our President.

Why is that?

I would suggest that it is because what this President is doing in El Salvador is consistent with what previous Presidents have done, since 1945, in Chile, Vietnam, Guatemala, the Dominican Republic and Iran. Three and a half decades of Bomb thought, of cold war, cannot have left the national mind undamaged; it is, after all, essentially corrupting to insist on carrying forward the ideals of democracy by denying its blessings to others. This is what Orwell in *1984* called the world of doublethink: "to know and not to know, to be conscious of complete truthfulness while telling carefully constructed lies, to hold simultaneously two opinions knowing them to be contradictory and believing in both of them."

The Bomb has organized our perceptions into a new world. For thirty-five years we and the Russians have been linked in a Manichaean system of state thought that may not, finally, be held accountable to the moral civilization of mankind. And just as we have had our precedents for El Salvador, they have had their precedents for Afghanistan and Poland, in Ethiopia, Angola, Czechoslovakia and Hungary. Each of the bomb-holding superstates has the demonic *other* to justify its espionage, its assassinations, its interventions and its invasions. They are totalitarian and we are democratic, they are a closed society and we are an open society, and we detest everything they stand for; but we and the Russians have actually created an unholy alliance, a gargantuan intimacy, in which by now our ideological differences are less important to the rest of the world than the fact that we think the same thoughts, mirror each other's responses, heft the same bombs and take turns committing crimes and deploring them, in some sort of alternating current of outrage and despair, outrage and despair which has with smoke and sulfur generated an ectoplasmic gel of objective reality along the lines of Orwell's tortured vision.

From the logic of Us or Them, a statist reality has been credited with its own culture, its own ethos, just as with only two digits, a one and a zero, the vast but always binary operations of a computer can simulate the infinite possibilities of real human intelligence.

We've got to *watch* ourselves. We are in thrall to our own Bomb.

We've got to watch out for the little explosions of nerve and fear in the constrictions of public debate, in the lassitude of our private lives, in the rising levels of irrationality, in our group relations, in the tendency of our elected governments to abridge our political liberties, in the pressure we feel not to dissent but to conform, to play it safe, to shut up.

Because the time may be approaching when we will have to choose between two coincident reality systems: the historical human reality of feeling, of thought, of multitudinous expression, of life and love and natural death; or the supra-human statist reality of rigid, ahistorical, censorious and contending political myth structures, which may in our name and from the most barbaric impulses disenfranchise 99 percent of the world's population from even tragic participation in their fate.

There is a Bomb and a culture of the Bomb, and we've got to dismantle them both.

You may trust that I wish, that we all of us here wish, this wasn't the character of our age or the nature of our obligation on this day of your commencement. We are all here under this tent, this most ancient of structures, and it is indeed possible it may rain for forty days and forty nights. But there is a chance that it may not. And that is my good news. The presumption of your collegiate life here, the basic presumption, is that every life has a theme. It is a literary idea, the great root discovery of narrative literature—every life has a theme and there is human freedom to find it, to create it, to make it victorious.

That is what your faculty wanted to say to you.

You are in charge of yourselves.

The stack of books you've collected in your four years here is an icon of the humanist ideal.

You have sanctity of thought, the means to stay in touch with truth.

Your living, inquiring and lighted minds are enlisted in the struggle for a human future and a society unbesieged by terror.

That is what your teachers wanted to tell you.

You may not have realized it, and we are somewhat embarrassed to have to say it, but willy-nilly and ipso facto, you commence this day in the name of civilization. ∎

SHULTZ AND PEN (1986)

A thousand writers from forty-five countries are convening this Sunday for the 48th International PEN Congress, the writers and poets organization founded by Amy Dawson Scott and John Galsworthy in England in 1921 and dedicated to the free expression of ideas and the enlightenment that comes of an uncensored world literature. Some of the visiting writers are Nadine Gordimer of South Africa, Jorge Amado of Brazil, Amos Oz of Israel, the Polish Nobel laureate Czeslaw Milosz, Margaret Atwood of Canada, Kobo Abe of Japan, Gyorgy Konrad of Hungary, Salman Rushdie of England, Günter Grass of West Germany and John Updike of the United States.

Also present to deliver an address at the opening ceremonies at the New York Public Library will be Secretary of State George Shultz.

Although a board member of the host PEN American Center, I have not been active in the planning or fund raising for this important occasion. I have attended no board meetings in the past year or so and am not acquainted with the thinking of those of my colleagues responsible for inviting Shultz to appear.

It is difficult for me to understand why he was invited. What has Shultz written? What is his connection to the world of letters? Has he been on the boards of libraries or publishing houses? Has he ever as Secretary of State championed the cause of universal free expression that so concerns the international community of writers?

At the last international congress held in the United States, in 1966, no member of the Johnson Administration was invited to address the writers. The late Ignazio Silone was heard then to remark what a pleasure it was to go to one of these congresses and not hear from the presiding politicians of the host country. Indeed, America is one of the few nations in the world in which writers don't have to ask for the endorsement of the government. I imagine the looks on the faces of the hundreds of foreign guests convened in the public library when they realize that American

PEN has put itself in the position of a bunch of obedient hacks in the writers union of an Eastern European country gathering to be patted on the head by the Minister of Culture. It is astonishing to me that my dedicated colleagues on the board would put in months and months of effort and do all that fundraising and planning merely to set up their fellow writers as a forum for the Reagan Administration. In those countries where governments hold firmly in hand and in power their own PEN centers, it is customary for august officials to welcome the PEN congress. One would have thought among all the messages to be sent to all the writers of the world, including those who will arrive and expect to be released for a few moments from the repressions of their homelands, that here in the United States we are free and independent and affirm our freedom and exercise it without fear of being thought irresponsible and disloyal by our political leaders. And that we don't need their imprimatur in order to get together to talk and eat and drink.

Shultz's government has been conscientious in its application of the ideological exclusion provisions of the McCarran-Walter Act, which keeps out such dangers to the Republic as the Nobel Prize-winner Gabriel García Márquez.

His government is so contemptuous of language as to insist that the bands of *contra* terrorists—whom it wants Congress to fund, and who wage war against civilians in

Nicaragua, killing men and women and children and mutilating their bodies—are "freedom fighters." This at once befouls our tongue and defames the freedom fighters of Hungary, who in 1956 with a few rifles and rocks and stones attempted to stop a Soviet invasion of their country.

Sunday at the PEN congress there will be several delegations of writers whose national intellectual communities have suffered considerable misfortune because of the policies of the Reagan Administration—the white racist government of South Africa, for instance, which this Administration has supported and identified with and which Shultz and the President have only reluctantly criticized, under pressure from Congress and the public. Writers both black and white have been tortured in South African prisons without a word on their behalf from Shultz. There will also be a delegation from our ally Turkey, which routinely imprisons and tortures its writers, and from the Chile of our friend Gen. Augusto Pinochet, whose sensitivity to poets writing of democracy and freedom can be compared to Hitler's sensitivity to Jewish intellectuals.

The charter of American PEN specifies that it is a nonpolitical organization. Certainly its protests on behalf of imprisoned and abused writers are objectively applied no matter what the ideology of the malfeasant government. Indeed, one of the best accounts of the abuses of human rights and free speech around the world is kept by the Freedom to Write Committee of the American PEN. Not a month goes by when it is not sending its fervent protests and appeals on behalf of writers imprisoned in countries whose governments Shultz just as fervently supports. Why then has the American PEN betrayed itself? It is more than a shame; it verges on the scandalous that those currently in stewardship of the American PEN and the 48th International PEN Congress should have so violated the meaning of their own organization as to identify it with, and put itself at the feet of, the most ideologically right-wing Administration this country has yet seen.

The next voice you hear, my fellow writers, will be Secretary of State George Shultz, who will address us on the values to a democracy of free speech and uncensored literature. ■

THE STATE OF MIND OF THE UNION (1986)

Those who talk to them and teach and publish them say that many of our young writers don't want to write so much as they want to be rich and famous. Literature is seen as an entry to the good life. This might be an amusing irony of passing interest except that if we go through SoHo and the East Village, we find the same attitude among young artists. They don't seem particularly dedicated to painting. Their passion is to make a big art-world splash and to do it as quickly as possible without working through to some kind of earned truth. Truth is phantom; reality is paint on canvas and dollar bills.

I'm not sure this spirit is unprecedented in Western civilization, but I think it is in America. And because I'm a writer I tend to regard my profession, in fact all arts and their practitioners, as our country's eye of light. It sees and can be seen into.

Where did this new attitude come from? Of course every writer I have ever known has been interested in money. They've talked about it, hustled for it, dreamed of it, stolen it and occasionally made it. But until now the best have let the world come to them, in patience or in hope or in bitterness, and whatever mad or cunning beings they've been, the doing of it has been the thing. They've written because they were helpless not to; they've written even at the price of their own destruction and the destruction of everyone around them.

The new attitude borrows something of the accelerated sense of life of the 1920s, when precocity and a daring irreverence caught up young people as the stock market had their fathers. But there is something unrecognizable here: it is not a spirit of selling out because it lacks that moral reference entirely; it is a kind of mutantcy, I think, a structural flaw of mind that suggests evolution in a social context.

What is that context?

The PEN American Center's recent hospitality to the writers of the world at the 48th International PEN Congress was lavish in the extreme. Under its president, Norman Mailer, some $800,000 was raised to feed and house and convene the visiting writers and to show them the city, from the Temple of Dendur at the Metropolitan Museum of Art, to the temple of Saul Steinberg on Park Avenue. A large part of the money was raised by a series of readings on Broadway: wealthy people paid $1,000 a seat for eight evenings of readings by older and celebrated American authors, including Mailer himself, Kurt Vonnegut, William F. Buckley Jr. and Woody Allen. Then, with the money in hand, Mailer invited Secretary of State George Shultz to address the opening session of the congress at the New York Public Library.

The dispute that invitation occasioned has been well publicized and needn't be reprised here. Mailer offered his critics two rationales for his action. The first was his hope, from some collegiality with power, to persuade the Reagan Administration to rescind the McCarran-Walter Act, which PEN views as a detestable and ludicrous impingement on the free movement of foreign authors and scholars across our borders. The second reason was expressed in the heat of the controversy before Shultz made his speech. He would have thought it obvious, Mailer said, that he had invited the Secretary because of the dignity his presence would lend to the proceedings.

That Norman Mailer wanted a touch of the scepter interests me. One would suppose that an international gathering of many of the best writers in the world needed nothing more for its dignity. For a writer, for an artist of any kind, the work confers its own dignity. Political endorsement should make a writer wary—as it did Robert Lowell, who in the 1960s turned down an invitation to the White House.

Nevertheless, PEN's congress lit the attention of the government, the media and the kind of people who almost nightly combine charitable impulses with having a good time. PEN has entry now to the glamour-charity circuit and can have more financing for its good works than it has ever had before. And so a poor, feisty writers' club gravitates to money and power.

Why is it I see in my mind at this moment the presiding smile of Ronald Reagan? We have watched Reagan reallocate the economic resources of this country, in an exponential leap, to military goods; we have watched him attend to the dismantling of legislation worked out historically from the moral logic of the Constitution and designed to make a more equitable society—the antitrust laws, the labor protection laws, the civil rights laws. We have watched him rouse from dormancy a new generation of know-nothings to affirm his covert racism and anti-Semitism, to raise hell with the books in school libraries and texts in grade schools and to support the ideological simplism of his foreign policy; we have seen his contempt for poor people on welfare and for environmental law, as if he thought, perhaps, that only poor people on welfare breathe air or drink water. But what will a historian of his Administration say of its peculiar effect on the intellectual and literary and academic life of this country, the specialized cells of the body politic that compose its spirit?

At the same PEN congress—an event of many illuminations—Günter Grass remarked during an exchange in which he referred to the condition of the South Bronx: "Why is it I cannot say anything these days in criticism of America without first giving assurances that I am not a Communist?" *The New York Times* reported this fairly but then, in a grisly confirmation of Grass's sense of where we are now, went on to mention that Grass is not known to have publicly criticized a Communist government in the past eighteen years.

The debasement of intellectual life in this country is perhaps more apparent to visitors than to natives because we see it only in its daily minutiae. We may even have become inured to the neoconservatives' standard reaction to dissent, which is to point a warning finger in the direction of the Soviet Union so we don't forget how free we are in our ingratitude. In their Manichaean view, to criticize American foreign policy vis-à-vis Nicaragua, for example, or South Africa, is to give de facto support to the Soviet Union. The corollary to this proposition is that we best preserve our freedom of speech by refusing to exercise it. As a bit of pure and simple Babbittry, this perception of self-criticism as a kind of betrayal or treason is beneath contempt; these days, though, it is not George F. Babbitt, the Midwestern salesman, expressing it but a significant branch of the intellectual community. That is a kind of news, is it not?

For some of our literary critics a political novel written by an American is likely to be "adversarial" and therefore esthetically flawed. One academic wrote a year or two ago that some of our well-known novelists (Mailer and Doctorow were two I remember in his citation) have as their raison d'être the undermining of the very society that has so well rewarded them. "Love it or leave it" was a hard-hat phrase in the 1960s. In the 1980s it is the taunt of the effete intellectuals coming from the heart of the academy.

The truth is that the Republic may have more to fear from the loss of overreaching ambition on the part of its young writers than from the errant ingratitude, if it is that, of the older ones. The loss of a social dimension in much of the otherwise impressive fiction being written today has been widely noted. Horizons have diminished. Today's novelists are technically superior to those of thirty and forty years ago, but they are less inclined to take on the big stories. Many of a season's novels will be harmonious with one another, as if everyone is sewing a great patchwork quilt.

Salman Rushdie was one of the many speakers at the PEN congress who noted that Americans seem unaware of the effect of the United States on the rest of the world. Others were less circumspect than Rushdie. They called our writing insular, naïve and provincial. The estimable John Updike defended us by reformulating in literary terms George Washington's conviction that this country should beware of foreign entanglements: he characterized his experience of the American state as a pastoral. The German writer Hans Magnus Enzensberger dryly commented that there seemed to be no recognition in Updike's Arcadia that the United States had the capacity, at its own discretion, to blow up the planet. Thus, positions were staked out in what is of course an ancient argument, which can never be resolved—the degree of political engagement necessary or desirable in an artist's work. Neither side of the argument will guarantee a good book. A great work usually reflects the entirety of the argument as it has oscillated in the mind of the writer. But that the argument should surface now, with each insufficient side of it divided fairly neatly between America and the rest of the world, suggests the possibility that we are suffering some state of mind not apparent to ourselves.

How could this national state of mind be characterized? If at its best the individual writer's mind is a democracy, where conflicting points of view are in constant struggle, and every truth has an answering truth, and every idea is subject to transformation; so at its worst the writer's mind can be the tyranny of one argument. I take the writer as the micro-nation. When, for whatever reason, a nation's myths—the prevailing beliefs of its ruling powers—go unargued and unexamined, the society's state of mind can be said to be tyrannical.

I have no empirical means of proving that such a state of mind exists in this country today. I am not a sociologist. I am not given to surveys; I don't take stock in polls or in journalistic overviews of the newsmagazine variety. My writer's mind thinks in images and makes connections in metaphor. So I will introduce here a fanciful notion, the possibility that our President is a resolved phantom of cold war, a kind of golem sprung from national premises and fears that have not been seriously examined in almost half a century. We have made him to protect ourselves from our enemies, but he has laid on us the burden of his inert spirituality. Even as he calls for reverence for life, even as he holds hands with ministers at prayer breakfasts, the dead weight of our times presses down on us. And the failure of the American artistic and intellectual community to separate itself, lift itself, from this phenomenon testifies to its unnatural power.

Everywhere in our culture these days the idea of progress is bashed and social action is scorned, from the Tory idea-plays that come from London to Broadway for critical raves and long runs, to the sophistries of racism in our sociological journals. The assemblage of brilliant Eastern European and Russian poets and writers and scholars who have emigrated here in the past ten years or so to write and teach has had great influence on our thinking. They are concerned lest we not learn from their experience. They warn us against the utopian impulse; they tell us that the desire for perfection is the source of all social woe. They have paid dearly for this knowledge but it is not American knowledge, it is European knowledge, with the terrible legacy of monarchal European history behind it. They look at us as innocents. They think our idealism breeds revolution. They see a legislative measure that presumes the responsibility of government to act equitably toward its citizens as incipient communism. They condemn as naïve and dangerously liberal a protest that our government is doing something immoral or cruel to another government. They misapply what they know. They forget or can't believe that insofar as revolutions go, ours is 200 years further along than the one they come from. The rest of us should be as wary of this particular foreign entanglement as we are of the more generalized foreign insistence that we become *engagé*, but we are not. Some of us join the shrill cry, others bury themselves in domesticity, while our golem stalks.

And what of our hottest school of literary criticism,

which takes the concept of ambiguity to new heights, or depths? A book is a text or artifact whose meanings are to be disentangled and put alongside one another for examination. This is a professional discipline worthy of a play by Molière. Its conclusion—that the author of the piece is finally of no consequence and that the illuminations of the piece are simply a matter of supracritical excitations—can be interpreted as meaning that the compositions of words have no or very little value. This is not too far from the conviction of illiterate teenagers who roam the streets and subways of New York with their ghetto blasters booming. At least they know they live in a postnuclear world.

Everything I've noted here, from the young writers impatient of a long creative life to the deconstruction of our critics; every variety of intellectual retreat, of conformism; every small loss of moral acuity, I see collectively as the secret story of American life under the bomb. We have had the bomb on our minds since 1945. It was first our weaponry and then our diplomacy, and now it's our economy. How can we suppose that something so monstrously powerful would not, after forty years, compose our identity? The great golem we have made against our enemies is our culture, our bomb culture—its logic, its faith, its vision.

That is my inflamed notion. Perhaps it can be tested in debate. That would be good. Now that it is out in the open, we might do well to move transversely in our search for meaningful reference, to leave Prague for Heidelberg, to put aside the golem and consider the story of Faust. Is it possible that the bomb, in its inventions and reinventions, is not primarily deterrence, or even a weapon at all, but an overwrought ambition, an impiety? After all, two of its progenitors, as students in Germany, were inspired one sunny day to think of getting something going in the laboratory approximating the nuclear reactions of the sun. And since men in high places now arrogate to themselves the right to begin a nuclear war, we should perhaps recognize that we have on earth a spiritual disaster of unprecedented magnitude. I look to the Catholic sensibility when I think of Faust and Mephistopheles: perhaps this sense of spiritual disaster is what the American Catholic bishops had in mind when they declared, in their pastoral letter, their opposition on moral grounds to any use of nuclear weapons. No emperor or fiend from the past—not Caesar, not Alexander the Great, not Attila the Hun—ever claimed the sovereign right to determine the life and future of the entire universe. Yet that power is now claimed by every graduate engineer who steps into a nuclear weapons laboratory. The original Faust had twenty-four years before the devil collected him. Mephistopheles is no more generous now than he was at the University of Heidelberg in 1509: our twenty-four years were up in 1969. It is fair to assume that he has been sweeping up his souls for some time now.

To wake up to the character of our culture is to struggle, with all heightened self-interest, to reassert our primacy in it. I appeal to the traditional values of self-aggrandizement for which we artists and intellectuals are supposed to be famous. The current state of mind of the union is intolerable if only because its discourse is not its own. It is the body's discourse. That fact alone should ignite our pride. We may then consider in our debate to come the idea that art in America has to find a postnuclear politics of transcendent diction.

Otherwise we might find ourselves, if we live, in the position the Hungarian writer George Konrad described to me at dinner one recent night. He was explaining why writers are so dangerous to the states of the Eastern bloc. There is no more Poland, he said. There is no more Romania or Czechoslovakia. They no longer exist. All that's left of each is a language and the stories and poems that carry it and the culture it recalls. The writers are the memory of the nations that once were, and therefore a threat to the states that pretend they still are. ∎

A CITIZEN READS THE CONSTITUTION (1987)

Adapted from a talk delivered by E.L. Doctorow at Independence Hall in September 1986. Doctorow announced that as a citizen-author he would examine the Constitution as something composed, as a text.

Not including the amendments, it is approximately 5,000 words long—about the length of a short story. It is an enigmatically dry, unemotional piece of work, tolling off in its monotone the structures and functions of government, the conditions and obligations of office, the limitations of powers, the means for redressing crimes and conducting commerce. It makes itself the supreme law of the land. It concludes with instructions on how it can amend itself, and undertakes to pay all the debts incurred by the states under its indigent parent, the Articles of Confederation.

It is no more scintillating as reading than I remember it to have been in Mrs. Brundage's seventh grade civics class at Joseph H. Wade Junior High School. It is 5,000 words but reads like 50,000. It lacks high rhetoric and shows not a trace of wit, as you might expect, having been produced by a committee of lawyers. It uses none of the tropes of literature to create empathetic states in the mind of the reader. It does not mean to persuade. It abhors metaphor as nature abhors a vacuum.

One's first reaction upon reading it is to rush for relief to an earlier American document, as alive with passion and the juices of outrage as the work of any single artist:

> We hold these truths to be self-evident, that all men are created equal, that they are endowed by their Creator with certain unalienable Rights, that among these are Life, Liberty and the pursuit of Happiness. That to secure these rights, Governments are instituted among Men, deriving their just powers from the consent of the governed That whenever any Form of Government becomes destructive of these ends, it is the Right of the People to alter or to abolish it, and to institute new Government.

Here is the substantive diction of a single human mind—Thomas Jefferson's, as it happens—even as it speaks for all. It is engaged in the art of literary revolution, rewriting history, overthrowing divine claims to rule and genealogical hierarchies of human privilege as cruel frauds, defining human rights as universal and distributing the source and power of government to the people governed. It is the radical voice of national liberation, combative prose lifting its musketry of self-evident truths and firing away.

What reader does not wish the Constitution could have been written out of something of the same spirit? Of course, we all know instinctively that it could not, that statute writing in the hands of lawyers has its own demands, and those are presumably precision and clarity, which call for sentences bolted at all four corners with *wherein*'s and *whereunder*'s and *thereof*'s and *therein*'s and *notwithstanding the foregoing*'s.

Still and all, our understanding of the Constitution must come of an assessment of its character as a composition, and it would serve us to explore further why it is the way it is. Here is something of what I have learned of the circumstances under which it was written.

The Background

The Constitutional Convention was called in the first place because in the postwar world of North America influential men in the government, in the Continental Congress, were not confident that the loosely structured Articles of Confederation, as written, could make permanent the gains of the Revolution. Without the hated British to unite them the states would revert to bickering and mutual exploitation. They had as many problems with one another as the classes of people in each state had among themselves, and men like George Washington and James Madison foresaw a kind of anarchy ensuing that would lead to yet another despotism, either native or from foreign invasion by the Spanish or again by the English. Many competing interests were going unmediated. The agrarian Southern states, with their tropical rice and cotton plantations, saw danger to themselves in export taxes applied to all their goods by the North Atlantic port states. The small states, like Delaware, felt threatened by their bigger neighbors, such as Pennsylvania. There was immense debt as a result of the Revolution, which debtors wanted to pay off with state-issued paper money—and which creditors, security holders, bankers, merchants, men of wealth, wanted returned in hard currency. There were diverse ethnic and religious communities, black slaves, white indentured servants. And there were Indians in the woods. The states not contiguous had little in common with one another. To a New Yorker, South Carolina was not the South; it was another kingdom entirely, with people of completely different backgrounds and with bizarre manners in speech and deportment—foreigners, in short. Georgia and South Carolina depended on slave labor to run their plantations. Slavery was abhorrent to many Northerners in 1781 and an economy of slaves was morally detestable.

It is important to remind ourselves in this regard that Colonial society had existed for 150 years before the idea of independence caught on. That's a long time, certainly enough for an indigenous class of great wealth to arise and a great schism to emerge between the rich and the poor. A very few people owned most of the land and were keenly resented. Three percent of the population controlled 50 percent of the wealth. People were not stupid; there was general knowledge of the plunder, legal chicanery, favoritism, privilege of name and corruption of government officials that lad created such inequity. In fact, it is possible that organization of public sentiment against King George is exactly what saved the colonies from tearing themselves apart with insurrections of the poor against the rich; that events like the Boston Tea Party and calls to arms by Jefferson and Tom Paine created the common enemy, the British, to unify all the classes in America and save, by diversion of anger and rage to the redcoats, the fortunes and hides of the American upper class. This was the class, as it happened, of most of the fifty-five men who convened in Philadelphia. Washington was perhaps the largest landowner in the country. Benjamin Franklin possessed a considerable fortune, and Madison owned several slave plantations.

There was an additional factor to make them sensitive. The convention had been called to consider amendments to the Articles of Confederation. The Continental Congress was even now sitting in New York City and doing government business, and not all that ineffectually. It was, for example, passing legislation outlawing slavery in the western territories. But rather than amending the Articles, the convention in Philadelphia was persuaded to throw them aside entirely and design something new—a federal entity that would incorporate the states. The agenda for this course of action was proposed by Governor Edmund Randolph of Virginia, who presented a number of resolutions for debate, and so it has come to be called the Virginia plan. But the sentiment for something new, a new federal government over and above state sovereignties, had the strong support of influential delegates from several venues. And so the convention got down to business that was actually subversive.

It violated its own mandate and began to move in the direction the federalists pushed it. It was because of this and because no one participating wanted, in the vigorous debates that were to ensue over the next months, to be confronted with a record of his remarks or positions, that the conventioneers agreed to make their deliberations secret for the entire time they sat, permitting no official journal of the proceedings and swearing themselves to a press blackout, as it were. That was to upset Jefferson greatly, who was off in France as a minister; the idea of such secrecy repelled him. Only Madison, fortunately for us, kept a notebook, which did not come to light until 1843 but which provides us the fullest account of those secret deliberations and the character of the minds that conducted them.

The Convention

What a remarkable group of minds they were. The first thing they did was constitute themselves as a Committee of the Whole, which gave them the power of improvisation and debate, flexibility of action, so that when the collected resolutions were decided on they could present them to themselves in plenary session.

Methodically, treating one thorny question after another, they made their stately way through the agenda. If something could not be resolved it was tabled and the next issue was confronted. Nothing stopped their painstaking progress through the maze of ideas and resolutions from which they slowly constructed a new world for themselves: who would make the laws, who would execute them, who would review their judicial propriety; should the small states balk at proportional representation, then the Senate would be created to give equal representation to every state. Some matters were easy to agree on—the writ of *habeas corpus*, the precise nature of treason. If one reads any of the dramatic reconstructions of their work, and there are several good books that provide this, one has the thrill of watching living, fallible men composing the United States of America and producing its ruling concept of federalism, a system of national and local governments, each with defined powers and separate legal jurisdictions.

Through it all Washington sat up at the front of the room, and he never said a word. The less he said the more his prestige grew. They had settled on one chief executive, to be called a President, and everyone knew who it would be. He had only to sit there to give the delegates courage to persevere. Franklin, too, lent the considerable weight of his presence, only occasionally saying a few soft words or passing up a note to be read by the speaker. Franklin was an old man at the time, over 80. At one point, when the proceedings were bogging down in dissension, he offered the recommendation that everyone stop and pray. The lawyers were so stunned by this idea that tempers cooled, probably just as he had intended, and the meeting went on.

And as the weeks wore on there slowly emerged among the delegates—or must have—a rising sense of their identity not only as Carolinians or Virginians or New Yorkers but as American nationals. A continental vision of nationhood lit their minds, and a collaborative excitement had to have come over them as day after day, month after month, they fantasized together their nation on paper. One cannot read any account of their deliberations without understanding how they made things up as they went along from their own debated differences, so that a sort of group intellect arose. It was wise with a knowledge of the way men act with power and from what motives. This objectification of separate personalities and interests came of a unanimous familiarity with parliamentary method and was finally self-propelling. These men invented a country of language, and that language celebrated—whether in resolutions of moral triumph or moral failure—the idea of law. The idea of a dispassionate law ruling men, even those men who were to make and effect the law.

Enough resolutions having been put forth, a Committee of Detail was formed to get them into an orderly shape, and that was accomplished with the scheme of articles, and sections under the articles, grouping the resolutions about legislative, judicial and executive branches, the rights and obligations of the states, the supremacy of the Constitution as law, etc.

When the Committee of Detail had structured the composition and it was duly examined and considered and amended, a Committee of Style was formed. That is my favorite committee. It comprised William Samuel Johnson of Connecticut, Alexander Hamilton of New York, James Madison of Virginia, Rufus King of Massachusetts, and Gouverneur Morris of Pennsylvania. Apparently Morris did the actual writing. And it is this document, produced by the Committee of Style and approved by the convention, that was called the Constitution of the United States. And for the first time in the various drafts there appeared in the preamble the phrase, "We the people of the United States," thus quietly absorbing both the seminal idea of the Declaration of Independence and the continental vision of federalism.

The Voice of the Constitution

So we come back to this question of text. It is true but not sufficient to say that the Constitution reads as it does because it was written by a committee of lawyers. Something more is going on here. Every written composition has a voice, a persona, a character of presentation, whether by design of the author or not. The voice of the Constitution is a quiet voice. It does not rally us; it does not call on self-evident truths; it does not arm itself with philosophy or political principle; it does not argue, explain, condemn, excuse or justify. It is postrevolutionary. Not claiming righteousness, it is, however, suffused with rectitude. It is this way because it seeks standing in the world, the elevation of the unlawful acts of men—unlawful first because the British government has been overthrown, and second because the confederation of the states has been subverted—to the lawful standing of nationhood. All the *herein*'s and *whereas*'s and *thereof*'s are not only legalisms; they also happen to be the diction of the British Empire, the language of the deposed. Nothing has changed that much, the Constitution says, lying; we are nothing that you won't recognize.

But there is something more. The key verb of the text is *shall*, as in "All legislative powers herein granted shall be vested in a Congress of the United States which shall consist of a Senate and a House of Representatives," or "New States may be admitted by the Congress into this Union; but no new State shall be formed or erected within the jurisdiction of any other State." The Constitution does not explicitly concern itself with the grievances that brought it about. It is syntactically futuristic: it prescribes what is to come. It prophesies. Even today, living 200 years into the prophecy, we read it and find it still ahead of us, still extending itself in time. The Constitution gives law and assumes for itself the power endlessly to give law. It ordains. In its articles and sections, one after another, it offers a ladder to heaven. It is cold, distant, remote as a voice from on high, self-authenticating.

Through most of history kings and their servitor churches did the ordaining, and always in the name of God. But here the people do it: "We the People . . . do ordain and establish this Constitution for the United States." And the word for God appears nowhere in the text. Heaven forbid! In fact, its very last stricture is that "no religious test shall ever be required as a qualification to any office or public trust under the United States."

The voice of the Constitution is the inescapably solemn self-consciousness of the people giving the law unto themselves. But since in the Judeo-Christian world of Western civilization all given law imitates God—God being the ultimate lawgiver—in affecting the transhuman voice of law, that dry monotone that disdains persuasion, the Constitution not only takes on the respectable sound of British statute, it more radically assumes the character of scripture.

The ordaining voice of the Constitution is scriptural,

but in resolutely keeping the authority for its dominion in the public consent, it presents itself as the sacred text of secular humanism.

I wish Mrs. Brundage had told me that back in Wade Junior High School.

I wish Jerry Falwell's and Jimmy Swaggart's and Pat Robertson's teachers had taught them that back in their junior high schools.

The Sacred Text

Now, it is characteristic of any sacred text that it has beyond its literal instruction tremendous symbolic meaning for the people who live by it. Think of the Torah, the Koran, the Gospels. The sacred text dispenses not just social order but spiritual identity. And as the states each in its turn ratified the Constitution, usually not without vehement debate and wrangling, the public turned out in the streets of major cities for processions, festivities, with a fresh new sense of themselves and their future.

Every major city had its ship of state rolling through the streets, pulled by teams of horses—a carpentered ship on wheels rolling around the corners and down the avenues in full sail, and perhaps with a crew of boys in sailor uniforms. It was called, inevitably, The Constitution or Federalism or Union. Companies of militia would precede it, the music of fifes and drums surround it, and children run after it, laughing at the surreal delight.

Of all the ratification processions, Philadelphia's was the grandest. There was not only a ship of state, the Union, but a float in the shape of a great eagle, drawn by six horses bearing a representation of the Constitution framed and fixed on a staff, crowned with the cap of Liberty, the words THE PEOPLE in gold letters on the staff. Even more elaborate was a slow-rolling majestic float called the New Roof, the Constitution being seen, in this case, as a structure under which society took shelter. The New Roof of the Constitution stood on a carriage drawn by ten white horses. Ornamented with stars, the dome was supported by thirteen pillars, each representing a state; at the top of the dome was a handsome cupola surmounted by a figure of Plenty, bearing her cornucopia. If you like the quaint charm of that, I remind you that today we speak of the *framers* of the Constitution, not the *writers*, which is more exact and realistic and less mythologically adequate.

Behind the New Roof came 450 architects, house carpenters, saw makers and file cutters, just to let people know there was now a roof-building industry available for everyone.

A thirty-foot-long float displayed a carding machine, a spinning machine of eighty spindles, a lace loom and a textile printer. There were military units in this procession, companies of light infantry and cavalry, and there were clergymen of every denomination. There were city officials and schools in their entire enrollments, but more prominent were the members of various trades, each dressed in its working clothes and carrying some display or pulling some float in advertisement of itself—sail makers and ship chandlers, cordwainers, coach builders, sign painters, clock- and watchmakers, fringe and ribbon weavers, bricklayers, tailors, spinning-wheel makers, carvers and guilders, coopers, blacksmiths, potters, wheelwrights, tinplate workers, hatters, skinners, breeches makers, gunsmiths, saddlers, stonecutters, bakers, brewers, barber-surgeons, butchers, tanners, curriers and, I am pleased to say, printers, booksellers and stationers.

So heavily weighted was the great Philadelphia procession with those tradesmen and artisans, it could just as easily have been a Labor Day parade. The newly self-determined America was showing its strength and pride as a republic of hard work, in contrast to the European domains of privilege and title and their attendant poverty system. The Constitution was America de-Europeanizing itself. A kind of fission was taking place, and now here was a working-class republic carried on the backs first of its citizen-soldiers dressed in rough brown and sober black, and then on the shoulders of its artisans and skilled workers. That anyway was the symbolic idea, the mythology that almost immediately attached itself to the ratified Constitution. From the very beginning it took on a symbolic character that its writers, worried always that they might never get it ratified, could not have foreseen. We speak of the "miracle at Philadelphia." That same impulse was working then: the celebration of the sacred text, miracles being beyond mere human understanding, a cause for wonder and gratitude—in a word, the supernatural.

The Subtext

Yet it is true also of sacred texts that when they create a spiritual community, they at the same time create a larger community of the excluded. The Philistines are excluded or the pagans or the unwashed.

Even as the Constitution was establishing its sacred self in the general mind, it was still the work, the composition, of writers; and the writers were largely patrician, not working class. They tended to be well educated, wealthy and not without self-interest. The historian Carl Degler says in *Out of Our Past*: "No new social class came to power through the doors of the American Revolution. The men who engineered the revolt were largely members of the colonial ruling class." That holds for the Philadelphia 55.

They themselves were aware of the benefits, if not to themselves then to their class, of the provision guaranteeing the debts incurred under the Confederation: the security holders, the creditors of America, stood to make a lot of money; at the same time, the debtors—the fret holders, the small farmers—stood to lose everything. It was a practical document in their minds. They did not think of themselves as founding fathers or framers or anything more august than a group of men who held natural stewardship of the public welfare by virtue of their experience and background. They were concerned to establish a free and independent nation, but also a national economic order that would allow them to conduct business peaceably, profitably and in the stable circumstances deriving from a strong central government.

The ideals of political democracy do not always accord with the successful conduct of business. Thus, as conceived in 1787 only the House of Representatives would be elected by popular vote. Senators were to be elected by state legislatures, and the President by an electoral college, meaning men like themselves who would command the votes of their localities. There was the sense in these strictures of a need for checks and balances against popular majorities. Furthermore, to come up with a piece of paper that diverse regional business interests could agree on meant cutting deals. One such deal was between the Northeastern states and the Southern. Importation of slaves would be allowed for twenty more years; in return only a simple majority in Congress would be required to pass navigational commerce acts that the seagoing Atlantic states much wanted. That odious deal appears, in part, in Article Four of the original Constitution. The exactness and precision of statute language in this case is used not to clarify but to euphemize a practice recognizably abhorrent to the writers:

> No person held to service or labour in one State under the laws thereof, escaping into another, shall, in consequence of any law or regulation therein, be discharged from such service or labour, but shall be delivered up on claim of the party to whom such service or labour may be due.

There is no mention of the word *slave*, yet a slave in one state became a slave in all. The Virginia delegate, George Mason, to my mind the great underrated hero of the convention, warned his colleagues: "As nations cannot be rewarded or punished in the next world they must in this. By an inevitable chain of causes and effects, Providence punishes national sins by national calamities." If you affect the scriptural voice, he could have been telling them, you had better aspire to enlightenment, or the power of prophecy of your speech will work against you. And so it came to pass. That odious article worked through a historic chain of cause and effect like a powder fuse, until the country blew apart seventy-five years later in civil war. Not until 1865, with the passage of the Thirteenth Amendment, was slavery outlawed in the United States. And the monumental cost in lives, black and white, of that war, and the cost to the black people, the tragedy of their life in the antebellum South, and to American blacks everywhere since then (the state poll taxes that kept black people from voting in the South were not outlawed until the Twenty-fourth Amendment was ratified, in 1964), shows how potent, how malignly powerful, the futuristic, transhuman Constitution has been where it has been poorly written. What was sacred is profane; there is a kind of blasphemous inversion of the thing.

In this formulation it is the power of the Constitution to amend itself, or, in writers' terms, to accept revision, that shows the delegates at their best. They knew what they had was imperfect, a beginning; Franklin and Washington said as much. Nevertheless, Mason refused to put his name to the constitutional document even after Franklin urged a unanimous presentation to the states, because of the slavery article and also because there was no Bill of Rights—no explicit statutes on the rights of American citizens to free speech and assembly and religious practice, and to speedy trial by jury of defendants in criminal charges; no prohibition against government search and seizure without judicial warrant; no guarantee of a free press and so forth. Alexander Hamilton argued that those things were implicit in the Constitution and did not have to be spelled out, much as people now say the Equal Rights Amendment is unnecessary, but Mason, to his credit, knew that they must be spelled out, which is to say written. Imagine where we would be today if Mason had not held his ground and if the lack of a Bill of Rights had not been taken up as the major concern of the antifederalists, such as Patrick Henry. We would be trusting our rights and liberties to the reading of the Attorney General, who today believes that people who are defendants in criminal trials are probably guilty or they would not be defendants, and who has said that the American Civil Liberties Union is essentially a criminals' lobby. George Mason's amendments, the first ten, were passed on to the states for ratification by the first elected Congress in 1791.

It is true of most of the sacred texts, I think, that a body of additional law usually works itself up around the primary material, and also achieves the force of prophecy. The Torah has its Talmud, and the Koran its *hadith*, and the New Testament its apostolic teachings. In like manner we have our sacred secular humanist amendments. Mythic or sacred time is endless, of course, and it was not until 1920, with the passage of the Nineteenth Amendment, that the women of the

United States achieved suffrage. (I am told that this amendment has still not been ratified by the state of Georgia.)

Hermeneutics

Notice at this point a certain change of tone: my song of the miracle of Philadelphia has wobbled a bit; my voice has broken, and here I am speaking in the bitter caw of the critic. Yet there is a kind of inevitability to this. One cannot consider the Constitution of the United States without getting into an argument with it. It is the demand of the sacred text that its adherents not just believe in it but engage to understand its meanings, its values, its revelation. One finds every day in the newspapers the continuing argument with the Constitution, as different elements of society represent their versions of its truth. President Reagan argues with it, Attorney General Edwin Meese argues with it, and so, as a defenseless citizen from a different point of view, do I. And, of course, the Federal judiciary has amended, interpreted and derived law from it. From the days of the great John Marshall on down—way down—to the days of William Rehnquist, the courts have not just worshiped the Constitution; they have read it. Their readings are equivalent to the priestly commentaries that accrue to every sacred text, and the commentaries on the commentaries, and we have

200 years of these as statute and opinion.

It is the nature of the sacred text, speaking from the past to the present and into the future in that scriptural voice that does not explain, embellish itself, provide the source of the ideas or the intentions from which it is written, but which is packed with wild history—the self-authenticating text that is pared of all emotions in the interest of clear and precise law-giving—it is the nature of such a text, paradoxically, to shimmer with ambiguity and to become finally enigmatic, as if it were the ultimate voice of Buddhist self-realization.

And so I find here in my reflections a recapitulation of the debate of American constitutional studies of the past 200 years in the same manner that ontogeny recapitulates phylogeny. Thus it was in the nineteenth century that historians such as George Bancroft celebrated the revolutionary nature of the Founding Fathers' work, praising them for having conceived of a republic of equal rights under law, constructed from the materials of the European Enlightenment but according to their own pragmatic Yankee design—a federalism of checks and balances that would withstand the worst buffetings of history, namely the Civil War, in the aftermath of which Bancroft happened to be writing.

Then in the early part of the twentieth century, when the worst excesses of American business were coming to light, one historian, Charles Beard, looked at old Treasury records and other documents and discovered enough to assert that the Fathers stood to gain personally from the way they put the thing together, at least their class did; that they were mostly wealthy men and lawyers; and that the celebrated system of checks and balances, rather than insuring a distribution of power and a democratic form of government, in fact could be seen as having been devised to control populist sentiment and prevent a true majoritarian politics from operating in American life at the expense of property rights. Madison had said as much, Beard claimed, in *Federalist* number 10, which he wrote to urge ratification. Beard's economic interpretation of the Constitution has ever since governed scholarly debate. At the end of the Depression a neo-Beardian, Merrill Jensen, looked again at the post-Revolutionary period and came up with a thesis defending the Articles of Confederation as the true legal instrument of the Revolution, which, with modest amendments, could have effected the peace and order of the states with more democracy than a centralist government. In fact, he argued, there was no crisis under the Articles or danger of anarchy, except in the minds of the wealthy men who met in Philadelphia.

But countervailing studies appeared in the 1950s, the era of postwar conservatism, that showed Beard's research to be inadequate, asserting, for instance, that there were as many wealthy men of the framers' class who were against ratification as who were for it, or that men of power and influence tended to react according to the specific needs of their own states and localities, coastal or rural, rather than according to class.

And in the 1960s, the Kennedy years, a new argument appeared describing the Constitutional Convention above all as an exercise of democratic politics, a nationalist reform caucus that was genuinely patriotic, improvisational and always aware that what it did must win popular approval if it was to become the law of the land.

In my citizen's self-instruction I embrace all of those interpretations. I believe all of them. I agree that something unprecedented and noble was created in Philadelphia; but that economic class self-interest was a large part of it; but that it was democratic and improvisational; but that it was, at the same time, something of a coup. I think all of those theories are true, simultaneously.

The 200th Year

And what of constitutional scholarship today, in the Age of Reagan?

Well, my emphasis on text, my use of textual analogy, responds to the work over the past few years of a new generation of legal scholars who have been arguing among themselves as to whether the Constitution can be seen usefully as a kind of literary text, sustaining intense interpretive reading—as a great poem, say—or better perhaps as a form of scripture. I have swiveled to embrace both of those critiques too, but adding, as a professional writer, that when I see the other professions become as obsessively attentive to text as mine is, I suspect it is a sign that we live in an age in which the meanings of words are dissolving, in which the culture of discourse itself seems threatened. That is my view of America under Reagan today: in literary critical terms, I would describe his Administration as deconstructionist.

And so, by way of preservation, text consciousness may have arisen among us, law professors no less than novelists, as in medieval times monks began painstakingly copying the crumbling parchments to preserve them.

All told, it is as if the enigmatic constitutional text cannot be seen through, but, shimmering in ambiguity, dazzles back at each generation in its own times and struggles. It is as if the ambiguity is not in the text but in us, as we struggle in our natures—our consciences with our appetites, our sense of justice with our animal fears and self-interests—just as the Founding Fathers struggled so with their Constitution, providing us with a mirror of ourselves to go on shining, shining back at us through the ages, as the circumstances of our lives change, our costumes change, our general store is transformed into a mile-long twenty-four-hour shopping mall, our trundle carts transmogrify into rockets in space, our country paves over, and our young republic becomes a plated armory of ideological warfare: a mirror for us to see who we are and who we would like to be, the sponsors of private armies of thugs and rapists and murderers, or the last best hope of mankind.

It may be that as a result of World War II and the past forty years of our history we are on the verge, as a nation, of some characterological change that neither the federalists of the convention nor the antifederalists who opposed them could have foreseen or endorsed. We are evolving under *Realpolitik* circumstances into a national military state—with a militarized economy larger than, and growing at the expense of, a consumer economy; a militarized scientific-intellectual establishment; and a bureaucracy of secret paramilitary intelligence agencies—that becomes increasingly self-governing and unlegislated. There may be no news in any of this. What may be news, however, is the extent to which the present Administration has articulated a rationale for this state of being, so that the culture too, both secular and religious, can be seen as beginning to conform to the needs of a national security state. More than any previous Administration this one apotheosizes not law but a carelessness or even contempt of law, as internationally it scorns the

World Court and domestically it refuses to enforce federal civil rights statutes or honor the decrees of judicial review, or gives into private hands the conduct of foreign policy outlawed by the Congress. And more than any previous Administration this one discourses not in reason and argument but in demagogic pieties. Its lack of reverence for law and contempt for language seem to go hand in hand.

By contrast, I call your attention to the great genius of the convention of 1787, which was its community of discourse. The law it designed found character from the means of its designing. Something arose from its deliberations, however contentious, and that was the empowering act of composition given to people who know what words mean and how they must be valued. Nobody told anybody else to love it or leave it; nobody told anybody else to go back where they came from; nobody suggested disagreement was disloyalty; and nobody pulled a gun. Ideas, difficult ideas, were articulated with language and disputed with language and took their final fate, to be passed or rejected, as language. The possibility of man-made law with the authority, the moral imperative, of God's law, inhered in the process of making it.

That is what we celebrate as citizens today. That is what we cherish and honor, a document that gives us the means by which we may fearlessly argue ourselves into clarity as a free and unified people. To me the miracle at Philadelphia was finally the idea of democratic polity, a foot in the door of the new house for all man- and womankind. The relentless logic of a Constitution in the name of the people is that a national state exists for their sake, not the other way around. The undeviating logic of a Constitution in the name of the people is that the privilege of life under its domain is equitable, which is to say, universal. That you cannot have democracy only for yourself or your club or your class or your church or your clan or your color or your sex, for then the word doesn't mean what it says. That once you write the prophetic text for a true democracy—as our forefathers did in their draft and as our amending legislators and judiciary have continued to do in their editing of its moral self-contradictions and methodological inadequacies—that once this text is in voice, it cannot be said to be realized on earth until all the relations among the American people, legal relations, property relations, are made just.

And I reflect now, in conclusion, that this is what brought the people into the streets in Philadelphia 200 years ago, those wheelwrights and coach-builders and ribbon and fringe weavers: the idea, the belief, the faith that America was unprecedented.

I'd like to think, in this year of bicentennial celebration, that the prevailing image will be of those plain people taking to the streets, those people with only their wit and their skills to lead them through their lives, forming their processions: the wheelwrights and ribbon makers, the railroad porters and coal miners, the garment workers, the steelworkers, the automobile workers, the telephone operators, the air traffic controllers, the farm workers, the computer programmers and, one hopes, the printers, stationers and booksellers too. ∎

A GANGSTERDOM OF
THE SPIRIT (1989)

Editor's Note: There is a tale behind the speech by E.L. Doctorow presented here. The following chronology should speak for itself.

May 21, 1989. E.L. Doctorow, nationally acclaimed novelist, receives an honorary degree and delivers the commencement address at Brandeis University's thirty-eighth commencement exercises. The summer issue of the *Brandeis Review* describes his speech as "provocative and sometimes disturbing." Also receiving a degree is Martin Peretz, Brandeis, '59, editor in chief of *The New Republic* and a Brandeis Trustee since 1976.

May 24. Evelyn Handler, president of Brandeis, sends Doctorow a letter telling him, "I have received only the most positive and enthusiastic comments regarding your address to the graduates."

May 24. John Hose, executive assistant to Handler, sends Doctorow a transcription of his commencement address and remarks:

> I hope you will take some pleasure in the knowledge that the number of requests we have already received for your remarks far exceeds the number of requests received in any previous year. With your permission, we should like very much to reprint the text of your Commencement Address in the fall issue of the *Brandeis Review*, a quarterly publication that is sent to all alumni, faculty, parents, and friends and supporters of the University.

July 6. Hose writes to thank Doctorow for permission to reprint the address and for returning the edited text.

August 6. President Handler sends Doctorow a small album of commencement photographs.

August 10. Doctorow receives a letter from Brenda Marder, editor of the *Brandeis Review:*

> Dear Dr. Doctorow:
> When John Hose, executive assistant to the

president, wrote to you about publishing your Commencement speech in the *Brandeis Review*, he was not aware that it is the magazine's policy not to reprint commencement speeches. Instead, we cover Commencement in the summer issue, showing the highlights in photographs and captions and often briefly paraphrase the keynote speaker's remarks.

As you probably noticed, there are many speeches and events on Commencement weekend. Given our space limitation, unfortunately we cannot cover them all. In addition, were we to begin publishing Commencement addresses this year we would be expected to publish them annually and, quite obviously, not all are of the same quality as yours…

August 16. The New Republic goes to press with its issue dated September 4, including a column headed "Cape Cod Diarist" over the byline of Martin Peretz. It begins as follows:

There is probably more nonsense uttered at commencement ceremonies than in Sunday sermons. I've had one piece of such nonsense ringing in my ears now for months. When I heard it from the mouth of novelist E.L. Doctorow I couldn't quite believe it. Well, I've now seen it in print, neither my ears nor my memory deceived me. Addressing graduates of a distinguished university, Doctorow told them that things had never been worse in America. For him, there was no golden age, merely a time when things weren't quite so awful.... It was an embarrassment to be on the platform with him, like having to be agreeably polite while some lunatic tells you he's Napoleon. Another honorary degree recipient sitting next to me put his head in his hands in disbelief.

September 4. Doctorow writes President Handler to ask "What has happened, Evelyn?"

> Just a day or two after receiving this [Marder's] strange letter, I found in *The New Republic* of September 4, an attack on my speech by your Trustee, Martin Peretz, who was present at the Commencement as another honorary degree recipient. Mr. Peretz characterizes what I had to say that day as "a calumny against America," which is odd because what I delivered was only a critique of the Reagan administration and right-wing Republicanism. Mr. Peretz' reasoning is of the fevered love-it-or-leave-it school, and quite consistent with the censorious

state of mind and current degradation of political discourse I described in the speech itself. But here's the point: Mr. Peretz mentions that it wasn't until he read my remarks in print that he was able to confirm that they were as distasteful to him as he had remembered. But, the piece not having been published, how is it possible that Mr. Peretz saw it in print? Were proofs pulled and sent to him? Is it University "policy" to clear what you run in the *Review* with Mr. Peretz? Is he the editor-in-chief of the *Brandeis Review* as well as *The New Republic?* Or do others of your Board of Trustees also serve as unlisted editorial overseers of what is permissible for the thirty or so thousand Brandeis alumni, faculty, and friends to read—of which political points of view are safe for the *Brandeis* community, and which are not? My dear Evelyn, you surely appreciate that I did not need to be published in the alumni magazine of Brandeis. But the implications of your change of heart in the context of what we both take to be the liberal humanistic ideals of higher education, are somewhat dismaying. What can I assume except that someone somewhere along the line found the speech too disturbing, too provocative, and that a distinguished university gave itself to the lamentable practice of self censorship? I expect you will have an explanation for this affront—not to me, but to a basic academic principle. I have arranged to publish the speech elsewhere—now that I understand how good it really is. But I will have to frame it in the circumstances of its suppression by the same university officials who sought me out, solicited me to deliver it, heard it, praised it, and asked for the right to publish it.

Collegially, E.L. Doctorow

Herewith, then, appears the unexpurgated version of Doctorow's commencement address. As a public service, we offer a complimentary copy to any Brandeis friend or alum who sends us a self-addressed, stamped return envelope.

Dr. Handler, members of the Board of Trustees, deans of the university, honored doctoral degree recipients, distinguished members of the faculty, parents, friends, and most especially the pride and point of these proceedings—the shining, resplendent class of 1989:

Good morning, class. You've been going to school all your lives, and in a few minutes you'll be free. But not until I've finished talking to you. I'm the last compulsory lecture of your undergraduate careers. I represent your faculty's last shot at you, their last chance to tell you what they meant, before you slip out of their grasp forever.

You know, a few miles away, not one but two heads of state are this moment about to address graduates like yourselves in a stadium seating 30,000 people. What they say will be of only theoretical interest to the young men and women somewhere in that crowd whom they are presumably there to address. Perhaps they will use the occasion to enunciate major foreign policy statements, and when they are through, they will get back into their motorcade with the Secret Service men running alongside, and lift off in their helicopters, and the TV cameras will shut down, and the army of reporters will scatter, and those students, at least the ones who didn't scalp their graduation tickets, will be able to look at one another and say: "Well, it *is* historic to see a President, but just what, after all, has been celebrated here?"

What, indeed?

It seems to me that your university this morning looks very, very good by way of contrast. Your president and faculty and Board of Trustees have presumed a commencement should be directed to the graduating seniors in an academic setting that retains its meaning and integrity—that what is being celebrated is the moment of your personal rite of passage, the moment of the beginning of your post-collegiate lives. And they know it's a crucial moment, a solemn celebratory moment, that should not be scanted; and so, I'm honored to be called upon to speak to you—not a politician but a writer, a novelist included, I like to think, among the "unacknowledged legislators of the world," in Shelley's phrase—you English majors know that—unacknowledged like the poets, like all artists, in fact, helpless legislators of created consciousness who from the struggles of their own minds make poems and stories that would contribute to the moral consciousness of their time.

So I will begin by turning for instruction to an earlier unacknowledged legislator, a story writer, a novelist, who lived and flourished in the 1920s. His name was Sherwood Anderson, and he's most famous today for a small book of stories about life in a small town in middle America around the turn of the century. *Winesburg, Ohio* is the title of this book. Some of you may know it. And in his introduction to the book, Anderson proposes a theory which he calls the theory of grotesques. It is not a scientific theory but a historical poetic theory of what happens to people sometimes as they strive to give value and meaning to their lives.

Here is the theory: that all about us in the world are many truths to live by, and they are all beautiful—the truth of passion and love, the truth of candor and of thrift, the truth of patriotism, the truth of self-reliance, and so on. But as people come along and try to make something of themselves, they snatch up a truth and make it their own predominating truth to the exclusion of all others. And what happens, says Anderson, is that the moment a person does this—clutches one truth too tightly—the truth so embraced becomes a lie and the person turns into a grotesque.

Suppose, for instance, you're thrifty and you work hard and scrimp and save and live modestly in order to pay your way through college. Your thrift is a good thing. But then afterward, in later life, long after it is necessary, you continue to deny yourself and you save and save until hoarding money becomes an end in itself. Your thrift has become a lie. You've turned into a miser. You've become a grotesque. You see how it works? If, for instance, your patriotism blinds you to all other moral and ethical truths, and from your love of country you deceive duly constituted bodies of governmental authority, and you break laws and shred documents, the truth of patriotism has turned to a lie in your embrace of it, and made you a grotesque. Or take the truth of self-reliance. It is undeniably beautiful. It was the truth that underlay the entire Administration of the previous president, Ronald Reagan—this idea of self-reliance, rugged individualism. Who wouldn't like to stand up for himself independently, and make his own way through life? Yet Mr. Reagan's advocacy of self-reliance caused him to scorn or forget other truths—of community, for example, and the moral responsibility we have toward those with fewer advantages, and the profound truth of the interdependence of all society's citizens. And so he was moved at various times in his Administration to take away school lunches for needy children and tuition loans from students, and to deny legal services to poor people and psychological counseling to Vietnam veterans, and Social Security payments to handicapped people. You see how it works—this theory?

In fact, I will venture to say that insofar as Mr. Reagan inserted his particular truth into the national American mind he made it the lobotomizing pin of conservative philosophy that has governed us and is continuing to govern us to this very moment.

The philosophical conservative is someone willing to pay the price of other people's suffering for his principles. And so we now have hundreds of thousands, perhaps millions, of our citizens lying around in the streets of our cities, sleeping in doorways, begging with Styrofoam cups. We didn't have a class of permanent beggars in this country—in the United States of America—fifteen or twenty years ago. We didn't have kids selling crack in their grade schools, or businessmen magnifying their fortunes into megafortunes by stock manipulation and thievery—I don't remember such epidemics of major corporate fraud. A decade ago you did not have college students scrawling racial epithets or anti-Semitic graffiti on the room doors of their fellow students. You did not have cops strangling teenage boys to death or shooting elderly deranged women in their own homes. You did not have scientists falsifying the results of experiments, or preachers committing the sins against which they so thunderously preached. A generation or so back, you didn't have every class of society, and every occupation, widely, ruggedly practicing its own characteristic form of crime.

So something poisonous has been set loose in the last several years as we have enjoyed life under the power and principles of political conservatism. And I have used Sherwood Anderson's theory of the grotesque to account for it, but I don't know what to call it—a gangsterdom of spirit, perhaps. I do know that to describe it is bad form. To speak of a loss of cohesion in society, a loss of moral acuity, is tiresome. It is the tiresome talk of liberalism. In fact, part of this poisonous thing that I'm trying to describe is its characteristic way of dealing with criticism: It used to be enough to brand a critic as a radical or a leftist to make people turn away. Now we need only to call him a liberal. Soon "moderate" will be the M-word, "conservative" will be the C-word and only fascists will be in the mainstream. And that degradation of discourse, that, too, is part of this something that is really rotten in America right now.

Some of you, perhaps some of your parents, may be wondering at this time if I am speaking appropriately for this occasion, which is after all a celebration. In answer, I have to say I believe my subject is all too appropriate; I think it is my obligation to tell you, as truthfully as I can, the context, the social setting in which you will find yourself when you walk out of here with your degree. As an unacknowledged legislator, I am giving you not a State of the Union Address but a State of the Mind of the Union Address.

What does it do to you young people, I wonder, to grow up in a time in which the bottom-line standard of business thinking now controls every aspect of our lives? You may have heard our President ask just the other day that the Senate delay its consideration of a bill to apply stricter ethical standards to government officials. Mr. Bush is worried that if men and women are made to behave honestly, they won't want to work in his Administration. That's funny, except that at one time people were *honored* to be called upon to use their expertise for the sake of their country. There was an ideal of public service, and financial sacrifice was part of that ideal. Now it is taken for granted by everyone in Washington that people can only be expected to come to work for their country if they can afterward turn a trick from it.

It is in this context that I find myself thinking of a lately deceased Brandeis graduate—as unbusinesslike a person as you'd ever meet. He is not the sort of alumnus you would expect to be mentioned or that I would expect to mention in a commencement address. His name was Abbie Hoffman. Class of '59. I knew Abbie, though we were not close, and I didn't have that much contact with him after the sixties. The truth is I found him easier to take from a distance; I have to admit that our ways were different, but I admired him tremendously. He was fearless, and very funny, with the humor, the precision of insight of a great political cartoonist. And as an activist he put his body on the line. In the sixties he was a scruffy sort of fellow, skinny and nimble, somewhat unwashed-looking with his torn T-shirts and jeans, his long hair, his headband. He was a founder of the Yippies, the Youth International Party. And he was in the vanguard of the antiwar movement in the days of big street demonstrations—much like the one they have been having in China, the students, these days, and for the same reasons—to bring government into alignment with the popular will of the people.

Anyway, Abbie did street theater, he staged events that might be clownish or vulgar but that invariably caught the attention of the media and enraged the authorities. (For instance, I remember he once wore a shirt made from an American flag, and when angry policemen tore it off his back he shouted, "I have only one shirt to give for my country!") He got people terribly mad, Abbie: He was insufferable. He was insufferable because he was the mirror wherein we saw ourselves. That's just what the biblical prophets did—they operated in just that way. Wasn't it Isaiah who walked abroad naked to prophesy the deportation of the Jews? And wasn't it Jeremiah who wore a yoke around his neck to prophesy their slavery? Same insufferable thing. So Abbie was a kind of unacknowledged legislator of this order. Once he organized a demonstration to ring the Pentagon and by means of prayers and incantations make it rise from the ground and levitate. And another thing he did—he stood in the gallery overlooking the New York Stock Exchange and threw handfuls of dollar bills down on the floor and watched all the traders scramble to pick up the money. These were prophetic acts, were they not? Throwing money onto the floor of the Stock Exchange knowing people would crawl around in a frenzy to pick it up? The Pentagon and the Stock Exchange are in the eighties the twin images of our idolatry. He had it exactly right.

It's my view that in the last decade or so of life in our country, roughly the time since you've been in the tenth grade, we have seen a national regression to the robber baronial thinking of the nineteenth century. This amounts to nothing less than a deconstruction of America—the dismantling of enlightened social legislation that had begun to bring equity over half a century to the lives of working people, to rectify some of the terrible imbalance of racial injustice and give a fair shake to the outsiders, the underdogs, the newcomers. We have seen the ideals of environmental sanctity sacrificed to the bottom-line demands of business thinking in which we have done only as much to protect our environment as industry has found convenient, as if only a few songbirds and some poor dumb animals were at stake, as if the bleeding hearts of woodsy environmentalists were the issue, and not our lungs and skins and genes, and the wholeness and health of our children and their children. We have seen a new generation of nativist know-nothings called up like primitive comic-book warriors to make overt the covert racism and anti-Semitism of the campaign demagoguery of our conservative politicians. And we have seen with more and more deadening frequency the banning of the books of our heritage in our schools and public libraries—as for instance in Panama City, Florida, where they have found it necessary to expunge such dangers to the Republic as *Wuthering Heights, Hamlet, The Red Badge of Courage* and *The Autobiography of Benjamin Franklin.*

So that we may have in fact broken down, as a social contract, in our time, as if we were not supposed to be a just nation but a confederacy of stupid murderous gluttons.

So that, finally, our country itself, the idea, the virtue, truth of America, is in danger of becoming a grotesque.

This is certainly serious stuff for a happy day, but I would not be doing honor to you and this occasion if I did not tell you what's been going on while we've been waiting for you.

That is something else I meant to say. That we've been waiting for you. Did you know that? Your mothers and fathers and grandmothers and grandfathers—in fact all the generations older than yours have been watching you and waiting for you. Because whether you know it or not, you have learned here at Brandeis the difference between athentic thought and cant, between the valid proposition and the fraudulent, between rational thought, honest perception, on the one hand, and simplistic intellectual flummery on the other. And that makes you very precious to us, and to our nation.

And if your teachers here have seemed to you at various times to possess commanding intellectual presence, and I trust they have, the truth is they are itinerants, like you, having given their lives over to the strange species-grooming that is peculiarly Homo sapient—the modest, exhausted instruction in mind-survival of the generations that will succeed theirs.

And everything impractical they've given you, lines of poetry, phrases of music, and philosophical propositions, and ancient histories, and myths and dance steps, is terribly practical—in fact, the only means we have of defending the borders of a magnanimous, humanist civilization—just that civilization which is today under such assault.

The presumption of your life here, the basic presumption, is that every life has a theme. It is a literary idea, the great root discovery of narrative literature—every life has a theme and there is human freedom to find it, to create it, to make it victorious. And so however you find your society as you walk out of here, you do not have to embrace its lies, or become complicitors to its cruelties. Perhaps that is what your faculty wanted to say to you.

You are in charge of yourselves.

The stack of books you've collected in your four years here is an icon of the humanist ideal.

You have sanctity of thought, the means to stay in touch with the truth.

Your living, inquiring and lighted minds are enlisted in the struggle for a human future and a society unbesieged by the grotesqueries of stupidity and error.

Yes, I think that's what your faculty might want me to tell you.

You may not have realized it, and we are somewhat embarrassed to have to say it, but willy-nilly and ipso facto, you commence this day in the name of civilization.

I have every confidence in you. And I congratulate you.

From up here I have to say you all look very beautiful to me. Your families, I know, are proud of you, your teachers are proud of you, Brandeis University is proud of you, and let me say as an itinerant speechmaker, I find that I am proud of you too. God bless you all. ■

AN OPEN LETTER TO THE PRESIDENT (1991)

Dear Mr. President:

When the United Nations voted sanctions against Iraq something quite unusual took place: A world congress made a virtually unanimous moral judgment against the depredations of a rogue state and then implemented its judgment with action. In international concert, troops were sent to guard Saudi Arabia's borders, and military means of interdiction, on the sea and in the air, were established to punish Iraq by economic strangulation. And it was the United States government, your Administration, that was the creative force behind this achievement.

I wonder why you don't understand what a great thing you accomplished.

This U.N. action, the first major cooperative international action since the end of the cold war, was not a mere repetition of previous instances of voted sanctions. Old alliances were breached, old animosities discarded. History has given us a moment to recognize and exploit a characterological change in the nature of the world order. Think of this ad hoc union of nation-states coalescing in the perception of a moral outrage and then taking a powerful noninvasive action to rectify it. There is a moral end—the restitution of what was stolen, the reconstruction of what was destroyed; and there is a moral means to achieve it—the withdrawal of economic fellowship. What makes this action resound is that it comes beneficently in a time of crumbling international real-political structures—when new structures take their being from the course of historical events. Whatever the motives of the allies backing your initiative, and whatever the inducements given them, almost accidentally there is a new united consciousness of nations that can begin to compose the civilized future.

War is an expedient of Saddam Hussein, Mr. President, because he is of the barbarous past. You have the chance to create a future in which, on a smaller and smaller globe, technology races to rectify the damage of earlier technology, and the needs of any one state are becoming the needs of all—air to breathe, water to drink, soil and climate to grow crops, and an unalienated, literate citizenry to advance the civilizations of a democratic planet.

In this light, it becomes tragically regressive to raise troop levels and think only with a military mind. A new period in history brings with it a new sensibility, and what is acceptable in an earlier age is understood as monstrous in our own. As we approach the twenty-first century, it is radiantly apparent that there is now no person on earth who has an inherent moral authority to send other people to their deaths. It is no longer philosophically possible. A chief executive is not a chieftain. Nor can he be a zealot.

There is a rumor going about that even as you've instructed your Secretary of State to visit Baghdad, the Quartermaster Corps of the Army has ordered 80,000 body bags. It was George Washington, in his prescience, who decided that holders of your office would be addressed as Mr. President. It was George Washington who decided we would not have kings. You do not rule by divine right. You are not ordained. You are a Mister. Unless you claim celestial lineage, you simply cannot elevate yourself to an ethical justification of a course of military action that may result in 80,000 dead American young men and women. Or 8,000. Or 800. I have not heard you say that our basic survival and identity as a nation are at issue here. It is no longer a chief executive's license to articulate a national interest, other than our basic survival, that requires the death of 80,000 young men and women.

The last time—another age, a distant past—something like that happened is celebrated now in austere solemnity, one might even think in the spirit of penitence, by that dark granite monument that sits with the names of the Vietnam War dead not far from your office. Tell me now to what end those soldiers died. What acute national interest did their deaths serve? We have hospitals full of those permanently maimed and paralyzed from that war. What real-political analysis of former Secretary of State Kissinger, now again urging blitzkrieg as one of the wise men of television, was borne out in the subsequent history of our security and comfort as a nation? Does he now say of the domino theory that he once so shrilly in his wisdom insisted upon that 50,000 of a generation died so that he can make the rounds at black-tie dinners? It is my understanding we have been talking lately to the Vietnamese about getting the remains of our MIAs home. There is something like normal diplomatic intercourse with these terrors of the Asian continent. And north of Vietnam there is still a Communist monolith government in China doing what Communist governments have always done, but as far as I can tell, you look on China now with a passion no more intense than a salesman's affection for a customer.

I wonder if you give yourself in any day the quiet hours of solitude that this situation requires. Do they let you alone? Do they give you time to think? Even to men with ordinary responsibilities, thinking is hard. Are you able to think? Do you make the mistake of assuming that having committed more than 400,000 troops to the desert you must, if your ultimatum is ignored, set them to fighting or lose face? I want to know whose face you would be losing. Do you delude yourself that it would not be a kind of criminal behavior to go to war to save face? I want to know whose face you would be saving. Nations are not people. Nations do not have faces—they have histories, they have constitutions, but they do not have faces. Perhaps you confuse the nation with yourself and have in mind your own face. But if I were a national leader I would welcome any degree of personal humiliation if it would preserve the life of one 18-year-old soldier. I would live content in everlasting disgrace if one paraplegic could get up and walk.

A modern nation's honor is not the honor of a warrior; it is the honor of a father providing for his children, it is the honor of a mother providing for her children. Surely that is the true meaning of the otherwise strange internal collapse of the Soviet superstate as well as the overthrow of its satellite governments of Eastern Europe—the universal perception of what, after all, twenty-first-century enlightenment demands.

But if you would still don the helmet, let me suggest that U.N. sanctions and embargo themselves constitute a military action. It is called a siege. As all military leaders from biblical times have understood, the siege is the most cost-effective of all military strategies. Without endangering one's own forces, it brings slow but inevitable doom to the enemy. He lives for a while on his own fat, and then he either surrenders or starves to death. And nothing need be negotiated with him because he is no longer in a position to negotiate.

I look forward with you to the day when Saddam Hussein and everything he represents is buried in the sands of the desert. All we have to do is stand here silently, in our armor, and watch it happen. And go on and see what kind of twenty-first-century world God has given us the opportunity to make. ∎

Yours sincerely,
E.L. Doctorow

ART VS. THE UNICULTURE (1991)

The following article was adapted from Doctorow's testimony to the House Subcommittee on Government Activities and Transportation in a hearing on oversight of the National Endowment for the Arts. At issue was language sought by Senator Jesse Helms that would have restricted the N.E.A.'s grant-giving process.

I'm a working writer. I pay attention to words, to what they mean and to the meanings beneath their meaning. Underneath this question before you today as to what conditions, if any, to attach to N.E.A.'s grant-giving charter, is a very simple principle, simple but apparently elusive or beyond the tolerance of those who are so quickly and sweetly outraged, those who would punish all voices not in harmony with their own—the crucial idea that we must protect the speech of those with whom we are least comfortable. There is no First Amendment principle involved in protecting the speech of those with whom we agree, those whose hands we want to shake because they represent our own beliefs and convictions. The principle emerges in the conflict and contention with ideas that offend us and with expression perceived to be in monumentally bad taste. At that juncture we define ourselves as a civilization that is free and proud and democratic, with trust in the national community's powers of judgment and analysis and in its ability to illuminate and finally discard ideas that are foul, destructive, malevolent or simply foolish—or we are fearful and constrictive and craven and without pride in the natural self-cleansing powers of a free society through which all ideas flow. Those who would limit artists in any way, in any medium, I call craven. Those who have not the courage of their country's constitutional convictions I call cowardly.

Now you may say, and it has been said, that there is no violation of free speech in the refusal to bestow a grant; that the artist can say anything he or she damn pleases—but if it's obscene, overtly sexual, pornographic or generally indecent by the usual standards, the artist cannot reasonably expect us to pay for making the art. This is solely a question of whether the government should pay for works of art that violate community standards of taste and decorum. This is a question of using hard-earned tax dollars to support the artist who mocks, sickens or otherwise offends the people who provide those tax dollars. That's all.

Of course, that isn't all. In the first place, as citizens we regularly see our tax dollars funding programs and policies and forms of speech we abhor—as for example when our taxes pay for presidential campaigns of candidates whose platforms are inimical to our interests and whose speeches offend our intelligence. We even see our tax dollars going to subsidize criminal enterprise, as illustrated so well by the S&L scandals. Why do we get so righteous about our tax dollars where artists are concerned? The U.S. government taxes its citizens on behalf of multitudes of services and functions it performs, some of them noble, some of them stupid, some of them destructive and shortsighted, some of them quite murderous—but in any event a hefty percentage of them in the face of the disapproval at any given time of a large segment of the tax-paying public.

Yet, this question always arises where artists are involved. Why? I suspect it is because those who would censor, those who would preen in umbrage, have no belief in the value to society of any kind of art, obscene or otherwise, unless it is from another age, with the artists themselves conveniently dead and gone. I suspect that behind this whole question of tax dollars is that practical man's vision of the painter, the writer, the dancer, the composer as a marginal member of society—that politician's gut sense of the artist as a luxury the society sometimes cannot and should not afford, who in most instances is something of a fraud, a sort of self-indulgent, self-aggrandizing deadbeat who performs no labor of any consequence but is nevertheless always making big claims for himself. I speak of the latent underlying jealousy we have for elevated expression that is personal, uninvited and powerful, that almost automatic anger we have for a kind of witness and truth-telling that is not endorsed or accredited by church, or corporation, or family, or other governing institution of our society.

This prejudice is profoundly in the American grain, and like all our prejudices it resists rational argument. Not all artists are good artists—very few are in fact great—but the work of independent witness, that often self-destructive willingness to articulate that which many may feel but no one dares to say, the blundering, struggling effort to connect the visible to the invisible, to find the secret meanings of places and things, to release the spirit from the clay— that rude, stubborn, squawking, self-appointed voice singing the unsingable—who we are, what we are becoming—is through all our regions and states and cities and schools and workshops and studios a natural resource as critical to us and our identity and our survival as are our oil, our coal, our timber.

To put restrictions on speech funded with tax dollars is itself to speak in a certain way, the way of pre-emptive state speech; it is to begin to create a realm of approved speech, an orthodoxy of discourse. To draw bounds around speech is to legislate, de facto, more speech to some than to others. And it is automatically to privilege the speech of those who would deny it to others. That is the truth that is lost in the current debate in Congress. The righteous desire to tell artists what they may and may not say is the instinct to monopolize a natural resource.

This is not an isolated issue you have before you about the workings of a minor government agency. It arises in a widening context in which, for example, this Administration has gotten a judicial ruling that does not permit doctors in federally funded birth-control clinics to mention the word "abortion"; a context in which the President has supported a constitutional amendment to limit free speech where the flag is concerned—a rare President in our history, to advocate a retrenchment in the Bill of Rights; a context that includes an exponential rise in the number of books banned from school libraries around the country; a context in which a self-declared neo-Nazi and former Ku Klux Klan leader has wide public support in his campaign for a governorship; a context, in short, and I say this knowing the courtesies of bipartisan inquiry may make you wince here, of racial and gender and ethnic divisiveness that proceeds directly from the ideas and values of the extreme right element of our two political parties. I ask you to consider this context—I ask you to consider these items I've mentioned as creeping increments of an official culture. I ask you to acknowledge as you think about our sinful artists that the agenda of the extreme right, just one element of our political spectrum, is what governs current political discourse—the questions we ask, the issues we raise, the problems we define—as it has for the past dozen years or so.

This issue we discuss here is created by an extreme conservatism as it wishes to organize our lives illiberally, in one mold, as a uniculture—a conservatism that has from its genuine but quite paranoid soul decided that there is no hope for this country except as all other political constituencies conform to its righteous ways. And so we have odd patterns of thought. College professors who object to racist inflammatory speech on their campuses are derided for being politically correct; at the same time, artists applying to the N.E.A. are subject to the criteria of political correctness.

It is irrelevant that community standards are violated by racist speech; but it is by upholding community standards that artists are denied grants. All this is quite odd. On the other hand, the conservative movement has never let the true meaning of words interfere with its political intentions. Our President speaks for civil rights but has repeatedly vetoed legislation that would relieve the inequities of racism. He reveres the environment but prevents laws from being enacted that would save it from despoliation. It's all very odd—and if you think I am wandering too far afield here, I remind you that we need every artist we have, every witness, just because things have become so odd, just because people in power don't mean what they say, because our public debate is so degraded, our political discourse so subject to intimidation and flimflam, that we need these strange people who go their own way, these artists. We need them. First we need to stake them to a few months' work, if they're good. And then we need to leave them alone.

I point out to you, if you haven't also already heard, the disbelief of the American people upon learning that in a week in which a man with a gun committed another one of our indigenous mass murders in a public place—twenty-three people dead, a new record—the Congress refused in its grim-jawed patriotic righteousness to pass a bill banning the sale of semiautomatic weapons. I want to point out to you the perception on the part of some of us of the ludicrousness of worrying at length about an artist's nudity or naughty words while granting murderous free expression to any maniac who happens to have the price of a gun and decides to walk into a restaurant and kill everyone he sees.

I'm a working writer and I dare call myself an artist. I do not feel marginal to this society but rather deeply involved in its practical working life. My work provides employment to others—editors, typesetters, publishers, binders, newspaper critics, booksellers, teachers, movie actors and directors, set designers and videotape store managers. Painters provide employment to printmakers, publishers, gallery owners and workers, art critics, TV documentarians, museum curators and museum guards. The work of artists in every medium provides jobs and stimulates the economy. The N.E.A. has generally funded younger writers at the beginning of their careers—so that they, too, presumably will be in a position one day to generate jobs for others. All artists are, economically speaking, small businesses. Perhaps we should be testifying before the Small Business Administration.

But in any event, I ask you not to accept the strange, alarmed, right-wing vision of things—it's bad not only for artists, it's bad for us all. Any legislative condition put on artists' speech, no matter how intemperate or moderate, no matter how vague or specific, means you publish a dictionary with certain words deleted from the language, it means you lay out a palette with certain colors struck from the spectrum. Do you really want to do this? Does the Congress in its wisdom really believe that bleeping out words, blacking out images, erasing portions of the tape, is what is needed to save this Republic?

I would venture to remind you by way of conclusion that if you give to Comstockery a little piece of your democratic or republican soul, it will next year demand a bigger piece. As politicians who know history you know that to appease this demon is to make it only more powerful and more voracious. It won't ever stop unless you stand up to it. For that reason, I urge you not to choose between more or less onerous grant-conditioning language. It is all censorship and I say to hell with it—it's nothing any decent American should stand for. Give the great N.E.A. back its original charter, in which there is no language requiring of artists political conformity in any guise. And you'll be able to go home to your families, and especially to your children, knowing you've done them, and your country, a great service. ∎

The Character of Presidents: Faith, Hope, and Voting (1992)

Mr. Bush has said, by way of defaming Mr. Clinton's character, that the character of a presidential candidate is important. So it is. The President we get is the country we get. With each new President the nation is conformed spiritually. He is the artificer of our malleable national soul. He proposes not only the laws but the kinds of lawlessness that govern our lives and invoke our responses. The people he appoints are cast in his image. The trouble they get into, and get us into, is his characteristic trouble. Finally, the media amplify his character into our moral weather report.

He becomes the face of our sky, the conditions that prevail. One four-year term may find us at reasonable peace with one another, working things out, and the next, trampling on each other for our scraps of bread.

That a President is inevitably put forward and elected by the forces of established wealth and power means usually that he will be indentured by the time he reaches office. But in fact he is the freest of men if he will have the courage to think so and, at least theoretically, could be so transported by the millions of people who have endorsed his candidacy as to want to do the best for them. He might come to solemn appreciation of the vote we cast, in all our multicolored and multigendered millions, as an act of trust, fingers crossed, a kind of prayer.

Not that it's worked out that way. In 1968 Richard Nixon rebounded from his defeat at the hands of Jack Kennedy, and there he was again, his head sunk between the hunched shoulders of his three-button suit and his arms raised in victory, the exacted revenge of the pod people. That someone so rigid, and lacking in honor or moral distinction of any kind, someone so stiff with crippling hatreds, so spiritually dysfunctional, out of touch with everything in life that is joyful and fervently beautiful and blessed, with no discernible reverence in him for human life, and certainly with never a hope of wisdom, but living only by pure politics as if it were some colorless blood substitute in his veins—that this being could lurchingly stumble up from his own wretched career and use history and the two-party system to elect himself President is, I suppose, a gloriously perverse justification of our democratic form of government.

I think of the President's men cast in Mr. Nixon's character: convicts-to-be Ehrlichman, Haldeman and Mitchell; and Henry Kissinger, who seemed to go through the ranks as if magnetized, until he stood at the President's side, his moral clone in the practice of malefic self-promotion. I think of the events sprung from Mr. Nixon's character: the four students going down in a volley of gunfire in the campus park of Kent State University. More than 7,000 antiwar marchers detained in a stadium in Washington, D.C. The secret bombing of Cambodia, the secret deaths, the secret numbers, the always secret *Realpolitik* operations. And one other lingers in the mind: the time he ordered plumed golden helmets, Bismarckian tunics and black riding boots for the White House honor guard.

The subsequent two holders of the office, Mr. Ford and Mr. Carter, showed hardly any character at all, the one a kind of stolid mangler of the language whose major contribution to American history was to pardon Richard Nixon, the other a well-meaning but terribly vacillating permanent-pressed piety who ran as a liberal and governed as a conservative. We jogged in place during their terms of office. Nobody in America can remember where they were during Mr. Carter's term, or what they were doing, or if they had any waking life at all. Mr. Carter's biblical fundamentalism gave him exceptional patience in the negotiation of a peace between Israel and Egypt, but Washington looked nothing like the Sinai and did not inspire him. The ancient Near East was his glory and, with the failed desert operation to rescue the hostages in Iran, his downfall. He did define human rights as a factor in international relations, but did not become an honorable champion of the idea until he had left office. His vapidity is remembered, like the nervous smiles flitting across his face, as an invitation to the electorate to bring in the wolves of the right who had all this time been pacing back and forth and fitfully baying in the darkness beyond the campsite.

And so in 1980 we found ourselves living the mystery of Ronald Reagan.

With not much more than his chuckles and shrugs and grins and little jokes, Mr. Reagan managed in two elections to persuade a majority of the white working/middle class to vote against their own interests. The old self-caricaturing B-movie actor had the amazing capacity to destroy people's lives without losing their loyalty. He was said to go blank without a script, and his political opponents could think of nothing worse to call him than, in the words of Clark Clifford, an "amiable dunce." But his heartfelt pieties and simplistic reductions of thought, his misquotations and exaggerations, his mawkish appeals to rugged self-reliance spearheaded a devastating assault on the remedial legislation that had been enacted from the New Deal to the Great Society, set off new brazen white racist furies across the land and culminated in the most dangerous conspiracy against American constitutional government in the twentieth century.

The old deaf actor who nodded off in staff meetings managed always to wake up in time to approve schemes at variance with his oath of office. He refused to enforce civil rights laws, subverted the antitrust statutes, withheld Social Security payments from disabled people, cut off school lunches for needy children and gave into private hands the conduct of American foreign policy in Central America. Under the persona of this fervent charmer, we were released into our great decade of deregulated thievery, and learned that the paramount issues of our age were abortion and school prayer, Meanwhile the rich got filthy rich, the middle class turned poor, the profession of begging for alms was restored to the streets and the national debt rose to about $3 trillion.

Now there was a President with character.

Since the end of the war in Vietnam, American government under Republican Presidents has been punitive. Their philosophy is called conservatism, but the result in these many years of its application has been to dissipate the wealth of the country and lower the standard of living, health and hopes of an education of all but the top economic stratum of society. That is punitive. What Mr. Clinton refers to, inadequately, as the trickle-down theory is really the oligarchical presumption that no one but an executive citizenry of C.E.O.s, money managers and the rich and well-born really matters. When Mr. Reagan talked of getting "the government off our backs" what he meant was freeing this executive from burdens of public polity. No regulatory agency must stand in the way of our cutting timber, no judge can enjoin us from acting to restrain the competition, no labor law must stop us from moving a manufacturing plant to Indonesia, where they work for a tenth of the wage. For that matter, women will have no legal rights in the conduct of their own personal lives, and the fate of all citizens, as well as the natural world they live in, or what's left of it, is to be entrusted perpetually to the beneficent rule of the white male businessman to whom God in His infinite wisdom has given the property interests of the country.

There is an electoral strategy for implementing this nineteenth-century baronialism, and we are seeing and hearing it again in this campaign because it has always been very effective. It relies on the mordant truth that the right-wing politician has less of a distance to go to find and exploit our tribal fears and hatreds than his opponent who would track down and engage our better selves. That it seeks out and fires the antediluvian circuits of our brains is the right's advantage in every election. Pat Buchanan at the Republican convention was the Cro-Magnon baring his canines and waving his club.

The right will always invoke an enemy within. They will insist on a distinction between real Americans and those who say they are but aren't. This latter is your basic nativist amalgam of people of the wrong color, recent immigration or incorrect religious persuasion. At the beginning of the cold war "fellow travelers" and "pinkos" were added to the list (Communists being historically beyond the pale). Mr. Nixon contributed "effete intellectuals"; Mr. Reagan's Secretary of the Interior, James Watt, threw "cripples" into the pot with Jews and blacks; and this President and his men have consigned to perdition single parents, gays and lesbians, and a "cultural elite," by which they mean not only the college-educated, cosmopolitan (Jewish and their fellow-traveling) residents of both coasts who write or work in publishing, films or television but really any person in any region of the country who is articulate enough to compose a sentence telling them what a disgrace they are.

Mr. Clinton's dissenting actions during the Vietnam

War place him at the head of the dark and threatening coalition of faux Americans. He is, finally, the treacherous son who dares to oppose the father. As far as Mr. Bush and his backers are concerned, when the young people of this country rejected the war in Vietnam, they gave up their generational right of succession to primacy and power. They could no longer be trusted. Neither could the democracy that spawned them like an overly permissive parent ever again be trusted. All the Presidents since Vietnam, from Nixon to Bush, have been of the same World War II generation. They will not be moved. The thrust of their government has been, punitively, to teach us the error of our ways, to put things back to the time when people stayed in their place and owed their souls to the company store.

In June 1989 Mr. Bush vetoed a bill that would have raised the minimum wage to $4.55 an hour over three years. In October 1989 he vetoed a bill that included a provision for the use of Medicaid funds to pay for abortions for poor women who were the victims of rape or incest. In October 1990 he vetoed the Civil Rights Act enacted by Congress to set aside Supreme Court rulings that make it more difficult for women and minorities to win employment discrimination suits. In October of the next year he vetoed a bill extending benefits to people who had exhausted their twenty-six weeks of unemployment insurance (reversing himself in November to sign a more modest extension). On June 23 of this year he vetoed a bill that would have allowed the use of aborted fetuses in federally funded research. In September he vetoed the family leave bill, which would have entitled workers to be allowed unpaid time off for births or medical emergencies in their families. In July he vetoed the "motor voter" bill, which would have allowed citizens to register to vote when applying for driver's licenses.

The would-be beneficiaries of these bills—people who sweep floors, kids who work at McDonald's, poor women, blacks, the critically ill, people who've lost their jobs, working mothers and fathers, and nonvoters (can't have too many of those)—always heard from Mr. Bush at the time of the veto that they had his sympathy, but that somehow, or some way, the bills on their behalf would not have done what they were designed to do and in fact would have made their lives worse.

Mr. Bush is a man who lies. Senator Dole, who ran against him in 1988, was the first to tell us that. Vice President Bush lied about his opponents in the primaries, and he lied about Mr. Dukakis in the election. President Bush lies today about the bills he vetoes as he lies about his involvement in the arms for hostages trade with Iran and continues to lie, even though he has been directly contradicted by two former Secretaries in the Reagan Cabinet—Shultz and

Weinberger—and a former staff member of the National Security Council. He lies about what he did in the past and about why he is doing what he is doing in the present. He speaks for civil rights, but blocks legislation that would relieve racial inequities. He speaks for the environment but opposes measures to slow its despoliation.

You and I can lie about our actions, and misrepresent the actions of others; we can piously pretend to principles we don't believe in; we can whine and blame others for the wrong that we do. We can think only of ourselves and our own and be brutally indifferent to the needs of everyone else. We can manipulate people, call them names, con them and rob them blind. Our virtuosity is inexhaustible, as would be expected of a race of Original Sinners, and without doubt, we will all have our Maker to answer to. But as to a calculus of damage then done, the devastation left behind, the person who holds the most powerful political office in the world and does these things and acts in these ways is multiplied in his moral failure to a number beyond the imagining of the rest of us.

Nevertheless, there is something hopeful to be discerned in all of this. Mr. Bush is a candidate on the defensive. His term in office has been disastrous. This presidential heir to the conservative legacy of Mr. Nixon and Mr. Reagan has about him the ambience of the weak dauphin.

His own right-wing constituency is disgusted with him possibly because he portends the end of an age, the decadence of a ruling idea or merely the played-out vein of the Republican gold mine. Certainly he is, in all his ways, less than resolute. Lying is a tacit admission of having done something inadmissible. A mosaic of presidential lies offers the cryptic image of a better world.

All else being equal, what sort of presidential character is most likely to take us there?

Who would not wish for someone, first of all, who realizes that once elected, he cannot be the President merely of the constituency that empowered him but, if he would fill the defining role of the office, a President on behalf of everyone? That is a simple grade-school concept, and, given the relation in America of money to politics, cannot be anything more than that. But the President who had the courage to live by it would immediately lead a reformist movement to erase the advantages big money accords to itself by its political contributions and its lobbying. This would presume a morally intelligent President as well as a courageous one.

I would wish for a developed historical sense in the President, one that could understand and honestly acknowledge that the political philosophy of what we lovingly call the free market has in the past justified slavery, child labor, the gunning down of strikers by state militias and so forth. I would want a presidential temperament keen with a love of justice and with the capacity to recognize the honor of humble and troubled people. And the character of mind to understand that even the borders of the nation are too small for the presidential service—that willy-nilly and ipso facto we're planetary blunderers now.

The true President would have the strength to widen the range of current political discourse, and would love and revere language as the best means we have to close on reality. That implies a sensibility attuned to the immense moral consequence of every human life. Perhaps even a sense of tragedy that would not let him sleep the night through.

Also, I should think he would be someone who really likes kids, who laughs to be around them, and who is ready to die for them—but who would never resort to the political expedient of saying so.

Perhaps Mr. Bush's major contribution to this campaign is his raising of the idea of character in the public mind. He cannot have thought it through: We've been living with him. We know his mettle. When a candidate is up for a second term we don't have to rely on his actions as a 23-year-old graduate student at Oxford to determine if he's got the goods. But it may be finally a great service to the electorate, and even a personal redemption of sorts, that he invites us to imagine by contrast with his own and his predecessors' what the character of a true American President should be. ∎

MYTHOLOGIZING THE BOMB (1995)

In 1943, with the war against Japan intensifying in the Pacific, Dr. L.F. Fisser of the National Defense Research Committee designed a tiny incendiary bomb for the use of the U.S. Army Air Force. The two-ounce bomb was to be dropped on Japan affixed to free-tailed bats (*Tadarida brasiliensis*), of which there happened to be an ample supply in Carlsbad Caverns, New Mexico. The bat bombs were to be chilled to hibernating temperature in ice-cube trays, packed 180 to a box and sprung free at a thousand feet above the ground, where they would thaw, and, in great hunger, swoop down on the wood and paper homes of Tokyo.

Something may be insane, but it is crackpot only when it doesn't work. Another plan to bring the total warfare concept to the Japanese capital was conceived by Gen. Curtis LeMay. Using B-29 bombers as they had not been used before, he sent waves of them in low over Tokyo at night armed with 100-pound oil-gel bombs and six-pound gelled-gasoline bombs. What came to be known as "the Great Tokyo Air Raid" burned out sixteen square miles of the city, leaving 100,000 people dead, a million wounded and a million homeless. Only the powers of the mobilized human imagination—powers that verge on magic—could transform a blind shrieking bat with a little bomb clipped to its skin into a B-29.

The Japanese government, at the time xenophobic and racist, its people self-persuaded of their subjection to a living God, had its own considerable powers of military imagination. The military thought not of bats to fight their war, but they did have an ample supply of young men who could be turned into bombs—human bombs, human torpedoes, human mines—to fly, to dive, to swim, perchance to explode, against enemy armament. This was glory. This was a culture of contempt for individual life. In battle, troops were ordered to commit suicide rather than surrender. It is no wonder, with such twisted regard for their own, that Japanese commanders were uninhibitedly brutal to their prisoners of war and to their subject peoples in China, Korea, Burma. They worked over 100,000 of them to death building their Thailand-Burma railway.

But the ways of death in war are innumerable. The ethics of warfare are reconfigured to its changing technology. By 1945 there was no longer a viable distinction between combatants and noncombatants. Perhaps 51 million human beings were killed in the worldwide war that raged from 1939 to 1945. Bombed, fire-bombed, strafed, mined, suffocated, gassed, incinerated, frozen, mutilated, starved, beheaded, hanged, buried alive and dissolved in a luminous flash. Certainly more than half of them died as civilians.

Twenty years before, another great war in Europe had killed its generation of young men, the fieldpieces drawn by horses, the ordinance in dinky trucks, though all of it sufficient unto the day, with Sten guns halving men on the dotted line, and mustard gas cauterizing their lungs, and some of those Big Berthas heaving 300-pound shells in seventy-five-mile trajectories. But the technology was not yet developed for carpet-bombing cities behind the lines. There were still lines. Civilians could still be refugees clogging the roads with their carts of bedding, their hope chests, their children, while the troops pushed through them toward the front.

That was the war before the war. The twenty years or so between the war before the war, and the war after the war before the war, were hardly riven by peace. The new fascist military states field-tested their machines, dive-bombing Ethiopians who carried spears and strafing peasants on horseback in Spain. The concentration camp and the gulag were invented, genocide was the subject of secret planning sessions, and Hitler was using radio for purposes of mass hypnosis.

And so we come to the perverse and bitter fate of the international community of theoretical physicists, who, swept up by the barbarities of the time, were driven out of Europe or inward to despair, and scattered among the nations that would once more war with one another. Their collegial exchanges of information were suspended. Their abstract considerations of the nature of the universe were suddenly and desperately practical. It became all too clear that the beauty of their calculations had hidden from them the terms of the truly Faustian contract they had somehow scratched their names to.

"Dear Sir," wrote Albert Einstein in a letter to President Franklin Roosevelt on August 2, 1939,

> Some recent work...leads me to expect that the element uranium may be turned into a new and important source of energy.... It may become possible to set up nuclear chain reactions.... Extremely powerful bombs of a new type may thus be constructed.... I understand that Germany has

actually stopped the sale of uranium.... That she should have taken such early action might perhaps be understood on the ground that the son of the German Undersecretary of State, von Wemacker, is attached to the Kaiser Wilhelm Institute of Berlin, where some of the American work on uranium is now being repeated.

America made the A-bomb out of fear of the A-bomb. Its components were either uranium isotopes or plutonium, high explosive lenses, bullets, tubes, steel frames, inner shells, outer casings, fins, neutrons, protons, radiant poisons and a dread of the malignant war-machined sociopathy of Adolf Hitler. Industrializing our fear, we were soon effecting controlled chain reactions under the field-house stands at the University of Chicago. Another year or two and we were thermally diffusing or extracting plutonium in Hanford, Washington, and Oak Ridge, Tennessee. We ran critical experiments at Columbia and Berkeley, and brought everything together for design and engineering at the secret community of brains in Los Alamos.

By 1944 the atom bomb was the employer of 129,000 people.

At the heart of it all, living in isolation at Los Alamos, the scientists and mathematicians and engineers enlisted for the enterprise worked long and hard hours on a two-track program, crafting one bomb that would have an internal firing mechanism to explode it, and devising a second that would implode. While they solved one design problem after another, the scintillations of their intellectual breakthroughs and discoveries were not always connected emotionally to the grim purposes behind them.

But of course they could never forget, and the work was not even finished before they began to say among themselves that the bomb must never be used. The energetic, chain-smoking Szilard, a Hungarian, began to circulate petitions. "Now I am become Death, the destroyer of worlds," said the presiding physicist and scholar of the Bhagavad-Gita, Oppenheimer, when the Trinity test at White Sands went off with blinding magnitude, like a born sun over the desert. Kistiakowsky called it the "nearest thing to Doomsday." Bethe, Peierls, Ulam, Rabi, all of them with such terrible sickening misgivings. And young Feynman, sitting over a beer, depressed, close to tears thinking of the number of people walking around at that moment who didn't know they were dead:

a ring of skull-bone fused to the inside of a helmet;
a pair of eyeglasses taken off the eyes of an eyewitness, without glass, which vanished, when a white flash sparkled

is the way the poet Galway Kinnell puts it. What is the mythic reference for such an event? Shiva? Prometheus?

The Tree of Knowledge? None is sufficient. Participating cross-mythically in cultures that encompass the globe, the nuclear explosion must itself become a primary myth in the postnuclear world to come. It will become a scriptural text. In this fiftieth-anniversary crop of serious books about the dropping of the bomb on Hiroshima and the second bomb over Nagasaki, and the world war they concluded, and the cold war thermonuclear Superbomb they generated, we see the lines beginning to be drawn, the lineaments of conflicting accounts, as when in the years of early Christianity the struggle began to turn history into gospel.

As this age goes on, if we have the time, we will choose according to the society we conceive for ourselves the scientists, politicians, generals and spies whom we want for our story. It will have Hiroshima and Nagasaki in it, of course; it will have the Berlin wall, Korea and the Cuban missile crisis. It will have Harry S. Truman. He came into the presidency with the death of Roosevelt in April 1945. The United States dropped its bombs in August, just four months later. We will argue among ourselves whether Truman made the crucial decisions or simply let the years of war planning and military momentum work out to their logical conclusion. We will argue about his need to come out from under the shadow of a predecessor of whose greatness there was no question in his mind. We will have to compute the most likely number of lives of American soldiers he saved by avoiding an invasion of the Japanese homeland. We will have to decide how much the desire to cow the Russians figured in his decision. We will eventually determine whether the bomb had to be dropped at all, and if there was the need for an invasion, given the wreckage of the Japanese war machine and the signals sent by Japan that it was receptive to negotiating a surrender. And if we decide the Hiroshima bomb had to be dropped, we will need to know why the Nagasaki bomb had to be dropped as well.

Examining the beginnings of the cold war, we will have to consider the character of Secretary of State James Byrnes, a South Carolinian and Truman appointee who insisted on making the bomb our postwar foreign policy and dismissed with fierce Southern contempt the international nuclear arms control advocates David Lilienthal and Dean Acheson. We will have to try to remember David Lilienthal and Dean Acheson.

If the atom bomb was fathered by Hitler, the hydrogen bomb belongs in part to Stalin—only in part because the arms race was as much a creation of our cold war containment foreign policy as it was a result of Soviet actions. At one point soon after the end of World War II, we were flaunting our atomic stockpile when in fact we had no assembled bombs and the work at Los Alamos had ground to a halt; and the Russians on their end were making ominous warlike references to their immense land armies when in fact they were an exhausted people with 20 million dead, a ruined economy and an infrastructure largely unrepaired from the German invasion.

Sitting on the other side of the world in Soviet Russia were the enemy's scientists, who relied on espionage reports to guide their research. Russian espionage was a major industry. During the early days of Lend-Lease they flew planefuls of technical information from Montana to Siberia—information from every conceivable field, including atomic research. Oppenheimer's counterpart was a Russian physicist named Vassilievich Kurchatov, who read the espionage dispatches with the acuity of a capitalist reading stock quotations. The Soviet counterpart to Gen. Leslie Groves, the director of the Manhattan Project, was the infamous Lavrenti Beria, Stalin's executioner and the head of the secret police, a fact of which the assembled physicists in their privileged dachas were only too aware. Their installation at Chelyabinsk was staffed with slave labor; their nuclear tests followed at regular lengths our tests at Bikini and Eniwetok. "Did it look like the American one?" Beria demanded to know once after a Russian blast.

The spies of the cold war were an assortment of idiosyncratic emissaries between the two cultures, a strange, furtive lot of usually young idealists, not terribly smart amateurs here—like Harry Gold and David Greenglass and, according to their testimony, Julius Rosenberg—and shrewder professionals in England, like Kim Philby and Donald Maclean and Guy Burgess. But the one who would most likely have a place in the postnuclear text appears now to be Klaus Fuchs, the young German Communist who was a superb scientist, a physicist of such repute that he worked in the inner circles both at Harwell in England and Los Alamos, from where he methodically leaked not only his own contributions but those of everyone else to his Soviet handlers. Vividly anti-fascist, he was personally drab, a joyless, unnaturally quiet fellow who contained in himself not only the scientist's torment of intellectual joy mixed with moral horror but the Soviet spy's anxiety of living dangerously in the West.

Richard Rhodes, in his exacting and compendious history of the hydrogen bomb enterprise, *Dark Sun*, says: "Knowledge derived from espionage could only speed up the process [of making a bomb], not determine it, and in fact every nation that has attempted to build an atomic weapon in the half-century since the discovery of nuclear fission has succeeded on the first try." That was not the general understanding of atomic secrets in the days of the cold war. Nobody was above suspicion. Much in the same way that Beria's scientists were told their past accomplishments would not protect them if they didn't continue to produce did the charismatic Oppenheimer—"Oppie," the gaunt, bony, blue-eyed genius who was the architect of the A-bomb—learn that in counseling against development of the H-bomb, he had committed a heresy for which he would be deprived of his security clearance. This was done in a public hearing that humiliated him and destroyed his spirit.

Testifying to deadly effect against him was his erstwhile physics colleague and friend, the brooding Edward Teller, once a strong advocate of international atomic controls but, at the time of his testimony, on the opposite course as the fervent promoter of—after himself—the H-bomb.

From the military ranks we will find ourselves looking more carefully at Gen. Curtis LeMay, who after his tactical successes with the B-29s in Japan went on to the task of building the Strategic Air Command and its fleet of B-52s, some of them always in the air, bombs aboard, to "kill a nation" if the need arose. He was a patriot. He was also a blunt, tough, sometimes reckless adviser. He was, above all, a von Clausewitz of the nuclear age. He realized that with atomic weapons there is no more time inside a war. As the bomb implodes, so does time. The years-long wars of the past are compressed to moments. Thus the mobilization for war must now and forever come before the war. It follows that this blood-besotted century, having with its technology erased the distinction between combatants and noncombatants, will continue, as in the cold war, to erase the distinction between wartime and peacetime.

On Elugelab Island on the northern end of Eniwetok Atoll in the Marshall Islands, on November 1, 1952, the hydrogen Superbomb, code name Mike, was fired half a second before 7:15 A.M. The blast vaporized the island entirely and turned every animal, bird and plant on the surrounding islands to cinder. The purplish fireball rose to 57,000 feet and eventually formed a canopy a hundred miles wide. "Its blast would have obliterated all New York City's five boroughs," reports Richard Rhodes. In "nanoseconds" it generated all the known elements of the universe and then created a new one. It was a thousand times more powerful than the Hiroshima bomb. It had a neutron density 10 million times greater than a supernova—"more impressive in that respect," a scientist observer said, "than a star." The critical difference between an atom bomb and a thermonuclear bomb is that atomic fission inevitably exhausts its own chain reaction, which puts a limit on the amount of destructive power that can be built into an atom bomb. A thermonuclear bomb fired with the element of deuterium is theoretically capable of being designed to go on to the nth power. The H-bomb has no known limits.

This means we are locked up and turning in space with

our Trumans and our Oppenheimers and our Fuchses and our Kurchatovs. We have closure. Until this story is written there can be no other. There is only one demand: that we select for our mythic archetypes just those scientists and politicians and generals and spies whose inadequacies of character put us most in awe of their immortal achievement.

It sits there now, conceptually finalized, a Superbomb of limitless capacity. A Runaway. It does not require a plane or a submarine or an intercontinental missile to deliver it. Whoever the enemy is, wherever he is, we need only set it off where we are. Behind a barn somewhere. In the backyard. ∎

BOOKS READ FOR THIS ESSAY

DARK SUN
The Making of the Hydrogen Bomb
by **Richard Rhodes**

CODE-NAME DOWNFALL
The Secret Plan to Invade Japan—
And Why Truman Dropped the Bomb
by **Thomas B. Allen and Norman Polmar**

JUDGMENT AT THE SMITHSONIAN
The Bombing of Hiroshima and Nagasaki
edited by **Philip Nobile**

HIROSHIMA IN AMERICA
Fifty Years of Denial
by **Robert Jay Lifton and Greg Mitchell**

WEAPONS FOR VICTORY
The Hiroshima Decision Fifty Years Later
by **Robert James Maddox**

HIROSHIMA
Why America Dropped the Atomic Bomb
by **Ronald Takaki**

CHILDREN OF THE ATOMIC BOMB
*An American Physician's Memoir of Nagasaki,
Hiroshima, and the Marshall Islands*
by **James N. Yamazaki with Louis B. Fleming**

ATOMIC GHOST
Poets Respond to the Nuclear Age
edited by **John Bradley**

F. Scott Fitzgerald
1896-1996
R.I.P. (1996)

Of that triumvirate of hero-novelists who came of age in the twenties, we may salute the big two-hearted pugilist, and stand in awe of the mesmerist from Mississippi, but it's the third one we mourn, the Jazz Age kid, our own Fitzgerald. His was the most natural and unforced of the three authorial voices; his plots required minimal invention. He rarely felt the need for fiction's sturdier tropes—a self-indicating style, extremes of action, the exotic setting—being disposed to work the high wire without them. He lived rashly, susceptible to the worst influences of his time, and lacking any defense against stronger and more selfish personalities than his own; and when he died, at 44, he was generally recognized to have abused his genius as badly as he had his constitution. Yet at his best, in *The Great Gatsby*, much of *Tender Is the Night* and the incomplete *The Last Tycoon*, he wrote nearer to the societal heart than either of his august contemporaries.

After his death, his friend and mentor Edmund Wilson made a selection of Fitzgerald's uncollected pieces, letters and notebooks, and published them with New Directions as *The Crack-Up*. It is instructive reading. The Fitzgerald of the autobiographical pieces is the chastened, mature man, sober, alone, with nothing to lose. He is writing in the Great Depression, but ignoring it except as the turn of events that has, not without justice, dropped him and his Jazz Age ways into the dustbin of history. In a time of bread lines and hobo jungles, and with totalitarian states rising all over Europe, somehow the young man who one drunken night leapt into the fountain at the Plaza cannot expect, still, to be everyone's idea of the great American author. But he can reminisce. He can remember the twenties—he can look back on his early success, or the New York of his youthful illusions, or his and his wife's years of sybaritic hotel hoppings, or the circumstances leading to his nervous collapse—and he can render them, bring them back alive for our consideration.

Not surprisingly, his tone is elegiac; the sense of a paradise lost infuses every line. But there is rarely a lapse into self-pity. And underneath all is the shrewd writer's assessment of his own rise and fall as a salable subject. The unstated presumption in the title essay, "The Crack-Up" (originally published in three installments in *Esquire*), is the author's still-lingering celebrity: That golden boy you all remember—see what's become of him.

Writing about himself or the changing manners and morals and social dynamics of the time that made him its symbol, Fitzgerald writes with clinical precision. At moments a poetic fever may take hold, when his metaphors stumble over one another in his determination to get through to his magazine audience, but he consistently offers the insights of a first-rate cultural historian. And whatever we say in criticism of him, we find that he has said it first. He is disarmingly confessional about his lack of sustained interest in the universal political crisis of his time, about the squandering of his literary capital in magazine hack work, about his life as a drunk, about his pathetic need always to prove something to somebody, about his snobberies and prejudices, all held with the passion of an *arriviste*. Everything we know about him, he knows about himself. And it turns out that all along he was haunted by his inauthenticity—whether as the young lieutenant in his

World War I overseas cap who never got overseas or as the urbane young author carried on the shoulders of his generation, "who knew less of New York than any reporter of six months standing and less of its society than any ball-room boy in a Ritz stag line."

Repeatedly he disclaims his role as spokesman and symbol of the Jazz Age, but by reflecting upon it from his chosen distance, he tolls its dreadful excesses in his own life, and so finds its meaning in the body of his wrecked career. There is gallantry in that. We begin to understand our particular affection for this writer. He lacked armor. He did not live in protective seclusion, as Faulkner. He was not carapaced in self-presentation, as Hemingway. He jumped right into the foolish heart of everything, as he had into the Plaza fountain. He was intellectually ambitious—but thought fashion was important, gossip, good looks, the company of celebrities. He wrote as a rebel, a sophisticate, an escapee from American provincialism—but was blown away by society, like a country bumpkin, and went everywhere he was invited. Ambivalently willed, he lived as both particle and wave. "The test of a first-rate intelligence," he wrote, "is the ability to hold two opposed ideas in the mind at the same time, and still retain the ability to function." And while he was at his first-rate quantum best, he used everything he knew of society—as critic, as victim—to compose at least one work, *The Great Gatsby*, that in its few pages arcs the American continent and gives us a perfect structural allegory of our deadly class-ridden longings.

The contemporary reader may have to work to understand the nature of the celebrated crack-up. Fitzgerald tells us that his "nervous reflexes were giving way—too much anger, too many tears." What can he be describing? A psychotic episode? Depression? A spiritual crisis? There is a muttering resolve in his account, a determination at the end to change, to be no longer available to the humiliations that have characterized his fate. "*Cave canem*," he warns those of us who would come importuning to his door. We have to smile in our sadness for our graying Jazz Age kid. Such bitter resolution is not characteristic of a breakdown, or the drained energies of the depressive. It is more the angry romantic's expression of inconsolability—in having had an innocence and, having lost it, having to mourn it. That progression of states of the American mind was prevalent once upon a time but now, at the end of this century of industrialized war and genocide, is itself to be mourned. ∎

IN THE EIGHTH CIRCLE OF THIEVES (2000)

Eased into governance by years and years of conservative ideology, the corporations of America today effectively oversee the Congress, the regulatory agencies and indeed the presidency itself. There is no Article in the Constitution that recognizes the supracitizenship of conglomerates; nothing is written that grants enlarged and pre-emptive voting rights to business organizations and their trade groups. But as Washington is run today, major issues of public policy are bent and distorted by these multiheaded Brobdingnags who bribe Congress with their money and coddle it with their lobbies, so that time and time again socially desirable legislation in the public interest, whether having to do with public health or safety, environmental protection, preservation of our natural resources or any other issue of clear relevance to the entire society, is defeated, sabotaged or transmuted by language into its perverse opposite.

Yes, you say, tell me about it. But this is the recurrent truth of Washington, so rhythmically repetitive as to be its heartbeat, the way it pumps. Corporations that pit themselves against the manifest needs of the American people according to the issues that arise take turns as enemies of the people. Nothing else on Capitol Hill occurs so reliably and regularly. It so prevails as a political fact of life that it is hardly news. It has been a long, long time since it was news. It is now only and obviously the way things are. Banking, oil, lumber, pharmaceuticals, weaponry, communications and electronics, chemicals, meat and poultry—whatever the industry, you'll find it striding with a proprietary mien through the corridors of power. But in the name of what kind of Constitution?

Apologists will cite the First Amendment, speak of the American or God-given right of people to function in their own interest. That is just what democracy is, they say, a raucous contention of interests that historically proves out as the genius of our system; it is what we have always done in this country right from the start, when frontiersmen in coonskin caps and leggings came to town, and later the men in cutaways and top hats, everyone, always, grabbing their representatives by the lapels and demanding to be represented.

But conglomerated organizations of capital are not exactly people. They are compositions of human talents formatted to their purposes. They are dedicated networks of artificial intelligence. They think and feel in numerical abstractions. They will advertise their employees as their human face, they will give themselves hearts and souls in their television commercials, but as institutions they are dimensionally beyond the humans who work for them or the shareholders who gamble in their stock. They transform themselves, take on or divest themselves of companies, move across national boundaries, restructure, wax and wane, merge with others of their ilk in an institutionalized dynamic that leaves even their executives irrelevant. They are profit manufactories that accumulate people or rid themselves of people according to the transhuman logic of their balance sheets. And for the loyalty they demand and receive, the quid pro quo is to absolve those working for them who act inhumanely on their inhuman behalf.

In effect corporate entities that function in Washington to achieve benefits for themselves—tax loopholes, contracts, entitlements, dismantling of regulatory acts—regardless of the overall social effect, pre-empt the idea of the larger community, the national ideal, the United States as the ultimate communal reality. A just nation is not envisioned but a confederacy whose people are meant to live at the expense of one another. Such social Darwinism finds the presumptions of democracy naïve. The corporations that will farm our lands, insure our lives and our health, finance our homes, entertain us, power our cars, light our lamps… ask only one thing in return: that we recognize two forms of citizenship, common and preferred.

How contemptuous this all is, what an enormous humiliation to a society of free people. We may ask those who speak of this corrupt and corrupting system as a kind of speech that mustn't be tampered with, if to privilege the free speech of corporations with vast treasuries on those grounds is not undeniably to squelch the speech of others who don't have the same resources. Or if, in fact, this huge application of money to the political process that so depreciates the power of the individual voter is not a de facto poll tax, with the expected minorities, Afro-American, Hispanic, joined in their disenfranchisement by the white citizenry.

To consider the elected politician in all this is to mourn the days when amateurism was part of the political culture. Somewhere along the line political officeholding became a profession. To keep working, politicians have regularly to come like buskers into the street, sing their song and dance their jig and hold out their hats. In the best of them, this ritual has to induce a degree of self-hatred. Television is the major reason campaigning is so monstrously expensive. The airwaves are owned by the public, but that is irrelevant to the broadcast licensees, who charge commercial rates for programming in the public interest… and then contribute heavily to campaigns, so that no one who is elected will get up in Congress and say what a swindle it is for the broadcasters to charge the public for the use of airwaves the public owns.

The fundraising dinners are affairs of the wealthy. If you are a politician, the fatter the check that comes in, the greater your indebtedness. Your conscience becomes an instrument of self-deception. Some politicians are entirely at ease with this, either because they are themselves wealthy and are one with their contributors, or so reliably conformed to the values of the plutocracy that they rise up fully banked—as for example the Governor of Texas, noted for his rigorous support for the death penalty and for the civil rights of heavily polluting industries, who miraculously appeared in all the papers two years before the primaries as a front-runner and who now floats atop a campaign fund of $80 million.

What kind of political culture does the politician cheerfully acknowledge, who can say, as Republican Senator Orrin Hatch has said, that to back reform of the system of campaign money raising would be an idiotic thing for his party because it collects more money than the opposition? What degree of public alienation can a politician like Senate majority leader Trent Lott depend on, who has brazenly said in sponsoring legislation written by corporate lobbyists that after all they are the specialists in their field, who know the issues better than anyone else? These are the remarks of senators confident of a general population so numbed and alienated that barely 50 percent of eligible adults bother to vote in national elections. These are the flaunted values of politicians who know of the conglomerate-owned press culture that there will be no editorial muckraking from the "in depth" journalists of the broadcast media; that the rampant corruption in Washington—the vast, deep and dangerous mutant character of the present state of things—will not be defined for what it is, and that who speaks of the bewildering broad front of failure and mendacity and carelessness of human life in so much of our public policy in tones any louder than muted regret will be marginalized for this indecorous transgression as a leftist, a bleeding-heart liberal or perhaps a raging populist, but in any event someone so out of the "mainstream" as not to be taken seriously.

How many in Congress today have the integrity, the strength, to distinguish the interests of their districts or their states from the interests of their heavy donors? How many think there is a difference? How many can honestly admit to themselves that the big money is their constituency? To hear the points of view of some of these people, how they have become so much the forces that have bought them, is to realize they are no longer guilty of hypocrisy, having been transmogrified.

The instructive image here is from Dante's *Inferno*, Canto XXV. We are in a pouch of the Eighth Circle, where the thieves are kept. A monstrous lizardlike serpent leaps onto one of the thieves, wraps its middle feet around his belly, pins his two arms with its forelegs and, wrapping its rear feet around his knees, swings its tail up between his legs and sinks its teeth into his face. And so intertwined, monster and thief, they begin to melt into each other like hot wax, their two heads joining, their substances merging, until a new third creature is created, though somehow redolent of both of them. And it slowly slithers away into the darkness.

Back in 1787, when the Constitutional Convention had done its work and the drafted Constitution was sent out to the states for ratification, the public's excitement was palpable. Extended and vigorous statehouse debates echoed through the towns and villages, and as, one by one, the states voted to ratify, church bells rang, cheers went up from the public houses and in the major cities the people turned out to parade with a fresh new sense of themselves as a nation.

Everyone marched—tradespeople, workingmen, soldiers, women, clergy. They had floats in those days, too—most often a wagon-sized ship of state, called the Union, rolling through the streets with children waving from the scuppers. Philadelphia came up with a float called the New Roof, a dome supported by thirteen pillars and ornamented with stars. It was drawn by ten white horses, and at the top was a handsome cupola surmounted by a figure of Plenty, bearing her cornucopia. The ratification parades were sacramental—symbolic venerations, acts of faith. From the beginning people saw the Constitution as a kind of sacred text for a civil society. Indeed, the voice of the Constitution is scriptural. It ordains. It empowers itself to give law endlessly into the future. Like the Bible, it requires interpretive commentaries that themselves have the authority of law because its principles must be applied to a multitude of situations. And where its prophecy has been false, as in the infamous Article IV, which made a slave in one state a slave in all, the national calamity of a civil war ensued before the text could be amended.

Today, the Constitution with its Bill of Rights and further amendments rules us with a set of behavioral prescriptions that, if we lived up to all of them, would make us a truly free and righteous people. When the ancient Hebrews broke their covenant they suffered a loss of identity and brought disaster upon themselves. Our burden too is unmistakably covenantal. We may point to our 200-some years of national survival as an open society, constitutionally sworn to a degree of free imaginative expression that few cultures in the world can tolerate; we may regard ourselves as an exceptional, historically self-correcting nation whose democratic values locate us just as surely as our geography and yet we know at the same time that all through our history we have brutally excluded vast numbers of us from the shelter of the New Roof, we have broken our covenant again and again with a virtuosity verging on damnation and have been saved only by the sacrificial efforts of Constitution-reverencing patriots in government and out of government—Presidents, senators, Justices, abolitionists, muckrakers, suffragists, striking workers, civil rights activists.

What is to be done now, when the Constitution is subjected to corporate-groomed politicians who read it as no more than a postmodern self-deconstructing text? The present wide-open, scandalous system of campaign financing is rationalized by a rightist ideology that portrays the federal government as stiflingly bureaucratic, intrusive and inimical to the natural rights of a free people. In the lifetimes of many of us the federal government has been just the opposite, a means of redress, redemptive justice and societal healing, as, for instance, when it enacted the Depression measures of the thirties and the Great Society legislation of the sixties. Today the corporate rightists in Congress mean to privatize the Social Security system, vouch the public school system out of existence and do whatever they can to limit if not decimate the regulatory agencies established to control their worst business excesses. By the logic of their thinking even the National Office of Weights and Measures could be construed as an impediment to business practices.

It is not that members of Congress—or indeed the media or the American public—are not aware of the inequity of the present money-soaked system of political life in our country. But to what extent that system is responsible for the grotesque distortions of our present priorities—with the resultant poverty of so many children; the way our jails proliferate for the incarceration of black men, with more and more penal systems run privately for profit; the drift into monopolization of our media and means of communication, with fewer and fewer megacorporations controlling more and more of what we read, see, hear or understand as the news; or the cost of health insurance policies that insure people until they get sick; the inequitable tax structure; the international trade agreements that rescind our environmental laws; the list is long—and how all of this is connected to the system of unrestricted and flamboyant political donations may not be always appreciated by the public or acknowledged consistently even by those members of Congress who have voted to reform the laws of campaign finance.

In fact, campaign finance reform as a phrase has been bruited about so long and to so little effect and is so yawningly dull, dreary and unresounding, it makes one wonder if it's not partly responsible for the conditions it has so far failed to address. Perhaps there is a basement office somewhere in Washington where mischievous lexicographers of a certain political orientation have the assigned task of finding the words and phrases to defuse the issues that threaten the interests of their employers. If so, campaign finance reform has done its work well. Because what is hidden in that modest little phrase is the vision of an honest, vigorously realized democratic republic.

To effect a true and thoroughgoing reform would not change the innately raucous competition of interests among us, but neither would it provide for the amplification of some of those interests to a level that is deafening. It would amount to a kind of revolution of our national political behavior; it would bring people of talent and vision into political life who are not now available to the nation; it would be breathtaking, predictive of a new authentic polyvocal Union; and with the possibility, at last, of addressing our entrenched social and economic inequities, the distortions of our priorities and what is grotesque about our public institutions, we would begin to come out of the terrible alienation that afflicts us and think again of the beauty of our national promise. We would hope to fashion ourselves more recognizably to the ideal of human rights implicit in our Constitution.

Perhaps, then, we should not rely on Congress to find the votes to pass a true and thorough reform bill that restores to us our dignity as citizens. A genuine ad hoc social movement may be required, a state-by-state struggle by referendum, issue-specific ratings at election time, an Internet-organized lobby to end all lobbies, but in any event something—some great public outcry to flatten back the ears of the distinguished colleagues in their paneled chambers.

To imagine such glory is to invoke the idealism of Walt Whitman. Whitman did not buy the elitist presumption of classic conservatism—that it was in the nature of some to lead and most to follow—even as it claimed to recognize its responsibility (as it does not now in its corporatized form) to look after, to take care of, as one looks after or takes care of children or pets. He saw it as a terrible depressant of human energies. He understood American democracy's breakout potential to enlarge the dimensions of human life, and thought that if the discourse was truly national, the communications omni-directional, the minds of a populace living in neighborly freedom could constellate into a universe that we hadn't yet dreamed of. That is why when he walked the streets of nineteenth-century New York, Whitman embraced everything he saw. He loved the multitudes, the industry of working people; he loved the ships in the harbor, the traffic on Broadway. But he was not naïve. He knew the newspaper business from which he made his living relied finally for its success on the frail shoulders of itinerant boys and girls, street urchins who lived on the few cents they made hawking the papers at every corner. Thousands of vagrant children lived in the streets of the New York Walt Whitman loved. Yet his exultant optimism and awe of human capacity was not demeaned; he could carry it all, the whole society, and attend like a nurse to its illnesses, but like a lover to its fair face.

And so must we. ∎

WHY WE ARE INFIDELS (2003)

We have lately been called infidels. Yet we are perhaps the most prayerful nation in the world. Both Tocqueville and Dickens when they came over here to have a look at us were astonished at how much God there was in American society. True, the infidel is not necessarily a nonbeliever; he may also be a believer of the wrong stripe. But I think, given the variety of religious practices in our country, including that of Islam, that the term infidel as it has lately been applied to us probably does not refer to any particular religion we may as a nation subscribe to but to the fact that we subscribe, within our population of 290 million, to all of them.

Of course most of our religions, including Christianity, Judaism, Islam and Buddhism, landed here at different times from other parts of the world. They have been vulnerable, as religions usually are, to such denominational fracture as to offer a potential parishioner a virtual supermarket of spiritual choice. Some of our religions—Mormonism, Christian Science, Native American anthropomorphism—were invented, or revealed, right here. And if we think even casually of the parade of creative and influential religionists on our shores—from the colonists Anne Hutchinson and Roger Williams, Jonathan Edwards and Cotton Mather to our citizen evangelicals Aimee Semple McPherson, Billy Sunday, Father Divine and Billy Graham—we notice immediately that we have left out the Adventists, the Millerites, the Shakers, Swedenborgians and Perfectionists of the nineteenth century, to say nothing of the stadium-filling brides and grooms of the Reverend Moon's Unification Church, or the suicidal cultists of Jim Jones, or the unfortunate Branch Davidians of Waco, Texas, or the Heaven's Gate believers who castrated themselves and took their own lives in order to board the Hale-Bopp comet when it flew past in 1997.

One of the less scintillating debates among theologians is on the distinction between a religion and a cult. But all together, our religions or religious cults testify to the deeply American thirst for celestial connection. We want a spiritual release from the society we have made out of secular humanism.

That our God-soaked country is, as political science, secular, may be indicated by the fact that the word for the state of being of an infidel, infidelity, brings to our minds not a violation of faith in the true God but a violation of the marriage contract between ordinary mortals. Philandering husbands and adulterous wives may be viewed as immoral and looked upon with contempt or pity, but they are not usually regarded as infidels. The term, however, may be justly applied to all of us, including the most pious and monogamous among us, because of a major sin committed over 200 years ago, when religion and the American state were rent asunder and all worship was consigned to private life. It was Jefferson who said, "Our civil fights have no dependence on our religious opinions, any more than our opinions in physics or geometry." And while it is precisely because of this principle of religious freedom that we enjoy such a continual uproar of praying and singing and studying and fasting and confessing and atoning and praising and preaching and dancing and dunking and vowing and quaking and shaking and abstaining and ordaining, a paradox arises from this expression of our religious democracy: If you have extracted the basic ethics of religious invention and found the mechanism for installing them in the statutes of the secular civil order, as we have with our Constitution and our Bill of Rights, but have consigned all the doctrine and rite and ritual, all the symbols and traditional practices to the precincts of private life, you are saying there is no one proven path to salvation, there are only traditions. If you relegate the old stories to the personal choices of private worship, you admit the ineffable is ineffable, and in terms of a possible theological triumphalism, everything is up for grabs.

Our pluralism has to be a profound offense to the fundamentalist, who by definition is an absolutist intolerant of all forms of belief but his own, all stories but his own. In our raucous democracy, fundamentalist religious belief has organized itself with political acumen to promulgate law that would undermine just those secular humanist principles that encourage it to flourish in freedom. Of course there has rarely been a period in our history when God has not been called upon to march. The abolitionists decried slavery as a sin against God. The South claimed biblical authority for its slaveholding. The civil disobedience of Martin Luther King Jr.'s civil rights movement drew its strength from prayer and the examples of Christian fortitude, while the Ku Klux Klan and other white supremacy groups invoked Jesus as a sponsor of their racism. But there is a crucial difference of emphasis between these traditional invocations and the politically astute and well-funded actions in recent years of the leaders of the movement known as the Christian Right, who do not even call upon their faith to certify their politics as much as they call for a country that certifies their faith.

Fundamentalism really cannot help itself—it is absolutist and can compromise with nothing, not even democracy. It is not surprising that immediately after the Islamic fundamentalist attack on the World Trade Center and the Pentagon two prominent Christian fundamentalists were reported to have accounted it a justifiable punishment by God for our secularism, our civil libertarianism, our feminists, our gay and lesbian citizens, our abortion providers and everything and everyone else that their fundamentalist belief condemns. In thus honoring the foreign killers of almost 3,000 Americans as agents of God's justice, they established their own consanguinity with the principle of righteous warfare in the name of all that is holy, and gave their pledge of allegiance to the theocratic ideal of government of whatever sacred text.

Not just on other shores are we considered a nation of infidels. ■

The Intuitionist (2003)

In the short run, I think, the intellectual satisfaction that came of doing criticism and philosophy as an undergraduate put a damper on the instinctive feeling I had for fiction writing. The rigorous instruction I received in the forms and structures and tropes of literary composition was all analytical and perhaps induced a degree of self-consciousness about my own aspirations. The great philosophical questions were by turns thrilling and humbling. The philosophical categories were immediately and permanently useful, but it was all too easy to lose oneself in the philosophical diction. So that as relevant and invaluable as my education would turn out to be to my life as a writer, I would not settle down to write my first novel until I was years beyond graduation, married, a veteran myself and in my late 20s. I did do some writing at Kenyon, but what I turned out was mere mental exercise. I had gone backward, away from all that natural surging need to express something, anything, to something else—if not backward then certainly up to the regions of the brain, to calculation, study, research, to the conscious application of learning, all of it wrapped tightly in the longings of the ego.

The truth of the matter is that the creative act doesn't fulfill the ego but changes its nature. As you write you are less the person you ordinarily are—the situation confers strength. You learn to trust what comes to you unbidden. You learn to trust the act of writing itself. An idea, an image, a voice, comes to you as a discovery, and you don't possess what you write any more than the mountain climber possesses the mountain.

Writers write by trying to find out what it is they're writing. The artist Marcel Duchamp was once asked why he gave up painting: "Too much of it was filling in" he said. The worker in any medium had best give it up if he finds himself only filling in what has been previously declared and completed in his mind, a creative fait accompli. It is not that you have no intellect when you write. It is not that you have no convictions or beliefs. It is that nothing good will come of merely filling in what you already know. You must trust the act of writing to scan all the passions and convictions in your mind, but these must defer to the fortuitousness of the work; they must be of it. A book begins as an image, a sound in the ear, the haunting of something you don't want to remember, or perhaps a great endowing anger. But it is not until you find a voice for whatever it is going on inside you that you can begin to make a coherent composition. The language you find precedes your intention or, if not, is sure to transform it.

By way of illustration I will dwell for a moment on how, accidentally, my first novel came to be written. After college, and after service in the Army of Occupation in Germany, I came home to write and found I could not. I constructed outlines for books, I researched outlines for books, I researched subjects for books, I intended to write books. And none of them got written. At this time I found work as a professional reader for a film company. The job called for reading novels and preparing synopses for the film executives who didn't themselves have time to read, or perhaps couldn't read, but were on the lookout for stories that could be adapted for the screen. In those days, in the late 1950s, westerns were very popular, and so it was given to me to cover one rotten western after another. Despairing of my failed efforts and the wretched pulp I was synopsizing, I thought of quitting. Then, remembering Henry James's admonition to the writer—to be the person on whom nothing is lost—I decided that I could lie about the West better than any of the writers I was reading. I put a piece of paper in the typewriter and typed "Chapter One" at the top, just the way writers in the movies do it. I had no plan, no outline, no research. All I had was the impulse to parody. But I had happened upon a wonderful geography book, *The Great Plains*, by Walter Prescott Webb. According to Webb there were no trees out there. It was something I might have known from seeing western movies with their mesas and cattle drives, but for some reason I found this fact immensely evocative, into my mind came the image of a vast, barren plain, a rock-strewn universe in which, in the distance, a few stick figures were trying to provide themselves a civilization. My desire to destroy the genre forever turned into a serious engagement with its possibilities: If I could write in counterpoint to its conventions, there would be parody, if not in tone then in structure.

All of this came to me in the instant of that image's realization. From the very first sentence I had the voice of the narrator and the situation in which he found himself. None of this was thought out in advance of the writing. I was able to write the book because I had not planned to, and because I was not qualified to, never having been west of Ohio. As a New Yorker I might even have thought Ohio was the West. It was a book that arose solely from the circumstance in which I happened to find myself. *Welcome to Hard Times* is the title under which it was published—a novel set in the Dakota Territory in the 1870s.

I will admit, baldly, that the reviews I received were good enough to certify me as a writer. I thought myself that I'd done a sound piece of work, that I'd pulled it off just as Kafka had in his first novel, *Amerika*, which he wrote without ever having left Prague. And then I received a letter from an elderly lady in Texas. She wrote in a fine, spidery hand, and she said the following: "Young man, I was with you all the way until your Mr. Jenks at his campsite out on the flats made himself a dinner of the roasted haunch of a prairie dog. At that moment I knew that you'd probably never been west of Ohio, because the haunch of a prairie dog wouldn't fill a teaspoon."

Called upon to defend the prerogatives of my art, I replied: "What you say, Madam, may be true of today's prairie dogs. But in the 1870s…"

In fact, Jenks's hunger might have magnified his measly portion into a dinner. But, right or wrong, I've let the line stand in all subsequent editions of the book. I am leery of perfection. In Hawthorne's great story "The Birthmark," a natural scientist insists on concocting a potion that will erase a birthmark from his beautiful young wife's cheek. He regards it as the one blemish on her perfection. Because she loves him, his wife drinks the potion. The birthmark slowly fades until her beauty is at last perfect. At that moment, she dies. And that's why I have left Jenks still out there on the flats having for dinner a roasted haunch of prairie dog. ∎

The White Whale (2008)

An address delivered at a joint meeting of the American Academy of Arts and Sciences and the American Philosophical Society on the theme of "The Public Good: Knowledge as the Foundation for a Democratic Society."

What does it say about the United States today that this fellowship of the arts and sciences and philosophy is called to affirm knowledge as a public good? What have we come to when the self-evident has to be argued as if—500 years into the Enlightenment and 230-some years into the life of this Republic—it is a proposition still to be proven? How does it happen that the modernist project that has endowed mankind with the scientific method, the concept of objective evidence, the culture of factuality responsible for the good and extended life we enjoy in the high-tech world of our freedom, but more important for the history of our species, the means to whatever verified knowledge we have regarding the nature of life and the origins and laws of the universe.... How does it happen for reason to have been so deflected and empirical truth to have become so vulnerable to unreason?

For some time now we have been confronted by a religiously inspired criminal movement originated in the Middle East that advertises its values by suicidal bombings, civilian massacres and the execution of arbitrarily selected victims by the sawing off of their heads. However educated, well-to-do and politically motivated the leaders of this conspiracy may be, they have invoked an extreme fundamentalist reading of their sacred text to mentally transport their rank and file back into the darkness of tribal war and shrieking, life-contemptuous jihad.

So that history, as we look to that part of the world, seems to be running backward, as if civilization is in reverse, as if time is a loop.

And here? The scientists this evening may have to correct me as I invoke the term "quantum nonlocality." As I understand the term and make metaphorical use of it, electrons shot from an atom will mirror one another no matter how far apart they are driven: a mile, ten miles, a hemisphere apart—you look at one and you have a reflection of the other, a kind of weird subatomic dance in celebration of the mimetic proclivities of everything in the universe, is quantum nonlocality.

This is not to suggest that our waterboarding and sensory-deprivation torture techniques, that Abu Ghraib and the incarceration in perpetuity without trial of terrorist suspects at Guantánamo, are the moral equivalent of 9/11. Only that a declared enemy with the mind-set of the Dark Ages throws his anachronistic shadow over us and awakens our dormant primeval instincts.

Apart from this uncanny synchronous spin, the domestic political fantasy life of these past seven years finds us in an unnerving time loop of our own making—in this country, quite on its own, history seems to be running in reverse and knowledge is not seen as a public good but as something suspect, dubious or even ungodly, as it was, for example, in Italy in 1633, when the church put Galileo on trial for his heretical view that the earth is in orbit around the sun.

I am not a scientist and don't deal in formulas, but as a writer I would, in the words of Henry James, take to myself "the faintest hints of life" and convert "the very pulses of the air into revelations." That surely provides me with a line to unreason. And so when I read that the President of Iran denies the historical truth of the Holocaust, and when I hear the President of the United States doubting the scientific truth of global warming, I recognize that no matter what the distance they would keep between them, and whatever their confrontational stance, they are fellow travelers in the netherworld.

Two things must be said about knowledge deniers. Their rationale is always political. And more often than not, they hold in their hand a sacred text for certification.

But, you may say, am I not narrowing this issue, politicizing it by speaking of our President? In this discussion of knowledge as a foundation for a democratic society, am I not misusing this forum to broadcast a partisan point of view? Albert Einstein once said that even the most perfectly planned democratic institutions are no better than the people whose instruments they are. I would translate his remark this way: the President we get is the country we get. With each elected President the nation is conformed spiritually. He is the artificer of our malleable national soul. He proposes not only the laws but the kinds of lawlessness that govern our lives and invoke our responses. The people he appoints are cast in his image. The trouble they get into, and get us into, is his characteristic trouble. Finally, the media amplify his character into our moral weather report. He becomes the face of our sky, the conditions that prevail.

From those fundamentalist leaders who proclaimed 9/11 as just deserts for our secular humanism, our civil libertarianism, our feminists, our gay and lesbian citizens, our abortion providers, and in so doing honored the foreign killers of nearly 3,000 Americans as agents of God's justice... to the creationists, the biblical literalists, the anti-Darwinian school boards, the right-to-lifer antiabortion activists, the shrill media ideologues whose jingoistic patriotism and ad hominem ranting serves for public discourse—all of it in degradation of the thinking mind, all of it in fear of what it knows—these phenomena are summoned up and enshrined by the policies of President George W. Bush. At the same time he has set the national legislative program to run in reverse as he rescinds, deregulates, dismantles or otherwise degrades enlightened legislation in the public interest, so that in sum we find ourselves living in a social and psychic structure of the ghostly past, with our great national needs—healthcare, education, disaster relief—going unmet. The President may speak of the nation in idealistic terms, but his actions demonstrate that he has no real concept of national community. His America, like that of his sponsors, is a population to be manipulated for the power to be had, for the money to be made. He is the subject of jokes and he jokes himself about his clumsiness with words, but his mispronunciations and malapropisms suggest a mind of half-learned language that is eerily compatible with his indifference to truth, his disdain for knowledge as a foundation of a democratic society.

It will take more than revelations of an inveterately corrupt Administration to dissolve the miasma of otherworldly weirdness hanging over this land, to recover us from our spiritual disarray, to regain our once-clear national sense of ourselves, however illusory, as the last best hope of mankind. What are we become in the hands of this President, with his relentless subversion of our right to know; his unfounded phantasmal justifications for going to war; his signing away of laws passed by a Congress that he doesn't like; his unlawful secret surveillance of citizens' phone records and e-mail; his dicta time and time again in presumption of total executive supremacy over the other two branches of government; his insensitivity to the principle of separation of church and state; his obsessive secrecy; his covert policies of torture and extraordinary rendition, where the courtroom testimony of the tortured on the torture they've endured at our hands is disallowed on the grounds that our torture techniques are classified; his embargoing of past presidential papers, and impeding access to documents of investigatory bodies; his use of the Justice Department to bring indictments or quash them as his party's electoral interests demand.... Knowledge sealed, skewed, sequestered, shouted down, the bearers of knowledge fired or smeared, knowledge edited, sneered at, shredded and, as in the case of the coffins of our dead military brought home at night, no photography allowed, knowledge spirited away in the dark.

Now, I realize that with these remarks I may be violating the linguistic proprieties of an academic convocation. I realize, in the tenor of these times, that anyone who speaks of the broad front of failure and mendacity and carelessness of human life in so much of our public policy, in terms any louder than muted regret, is usually marginalized as some sort of radical—that is, as someone so "out of the mainstream" as not to be taken seriously. But I believe what I have described so far is an accurate and informed account of the present state of the Union.

We must ask if this rage to deconstruct the Constitution and the Bill of Rights has any connection with the prevalence of God in the mind of this worshipful President. We must ask to what extent, and at however unconscious a level, a conflict arises in the pious political mind when it is sworn to uphold the civil religion of the Constitution.

The idea of the United States may have had its sources in the European Enlightenment, but it was the actions taken by self-declared Americans that brought it into focus and established it as an entity. America is a society evolved from words written down on paper by ordinary mortals, however extraordinary they happened to be as human beings. When constitutional scholars speak of the American civil religion, they recognize that along with its separation of church and state our Constitution and its amendments establish as civil law ethical presumptions common to Judaism, Christianity and Islam.

But if you have extracted the basic ethics of religious invention and found the mechanism for installing them in the statutes of the secular civic order, but have consigned all the doctrine and rite and ritual, all the symbols and traditional practices, to the precincts of private life, you are saying there is no one proven path to salvation, there are only traditions. If you relegate the old stories to the personal choices of private worship, you admit that the ineffable is ineffable, and in terms of a possible theological triumphalism, everything is up for grabs.

Our pluralism cannot be entirely comfortable to someone of evangelical faith. But to the extreme fundamentalist—that member of the evangelical community militant in his belief, an absolutist intolerant of all forms of belief but his own, all stories but his own—our pluralism has to be a profound offense. I speak of the so-called "political base" with which our President has bonded. In our raucous democracy, fundamentalist religious belief has organized itself with political acumen to promulgate law that would undermine just those secular humanist principles that encourage it to flourish in freedom. Of course, there has rarely been a period in our history when God has not been called upon to march. Northern abolitionists and Southern slave owners both claimed biblical endorsement. Martin Luther King Jr.'s civil rights movement drew its strength from prayer and examples of Christian fortitude, while the Ku Klux Klan invoked Jesus as a sponsor of its racism. But there is a crucial difference between these traditional invocations and the politically astute and well-funded activists of today's Christian right who do not call upon their faith to certify their politics as much as they call for a country that certifies their faith.

Fundamentalism really cannot help itself—it is absolutist and can compromise with nothing, not even democracy.

I value the point of view of Professor Mark Noll, who speaks of the "historical American merger of the forces of traditional Christianity with the forces of Enlightenment." It is a serious misreading of American history, he says, "to portray the tangled cultural and political conflicts of our time as pitting the pre-critical hordes of religion against the hyper-critical avatars of science." Historically there has tended to be a religious accommodation of science, according to Professor Noll: in nineteenth-century America, theological conservatives could also be Darwinists. And even in the strident debates of today, fundamentalists still proclaim their allegiance to facts as loudly as their opponents. And theories such as intelligent design and creation science implicitly accept the modern scientific consensus on evolution while maintaining a confident belief in a traditional deity.

But all contrarian movements, like revolutions, devolve to their extremist expression, do they not? The theorists of creation science and intelligent design have marching on their right flank, with or without their approval, if not pre-critical hordes of religion, a militantly censorious, well-funded political movement that a President of the United States has tapped into for his and their benefit. I am not aware that American history as invoked by Professor Noll has a precedent for this. Nor am I aware that the hypercritical avatars of the secular scientific method have an equivalent hard-nosed political organization behind them.

The President has said the war with terrorists will last for decades and is a confrontation between "good and evil." Whether he means the evil of specific terrorist organizations or the culture from which they spring, his vision is necessarily Manichaean. There is immense political power in such religiously inspired reductionism. Thus, no matter how he lies about the reason for his invasion of Iraq, or how badly it has gone, bumblingly and tragically ruinous, with so many lives destroyed, and no matter how many thousands of terrorists it has brought into being, to criticize his policy or the architects of it is said to aid the enemy. The President's inner circle of advisers, who conspire in this Manichaean worldview, have the unnatural vividness of personality of Shakespearean plotters. While the original think-tank theorists and proponents of the war have quietly and understandably withdrawn from public view, the Vice President and the President's chief policy adviser have stood tall—the first contemptuous of his critics, his denials of reality and obfuscations delivered in the dour tones of unquestionable authority, the second too clever by half, and because he spent his years developing a theocratic constituency and wearing such blinders as an exclusive concern with party power has attached to him, most clearly has a future in the culture of antidemocracy he has so deviously and unwisely nurtured.

A Manichaean politics reduces the relevance of knowledge and degrades the truth that knowledge discovers. The past seven years of American political life are an uncanny cycle we've slipped into, or slid into, that foresees the democratic traditions of this country as too much of a luxury to be maintained. We have seen, since the 2006 election, the struggle for the legislative branches to regain some of their constitutional prerogatives. They struggle not only with a recalcitrant President and Vice President who impugn their motives but against the precedents of the imperial presidencies of Richard Nixon and Ronald Reagan, each of whom added another conservative shock to the principle of separation of powers. Many of the executive practices today—the blatant cronyism, the political uses of the Justice Department, the evisceration of regulatory agencies and so on—are empowered by these precedents. And so we have marched along from the imperial presidency to the borders of authoritarianism.

To take the long view, American politics may be seen as the struggle between the idealistic secular democracy of a fearlessly self-renewing America and our great resident capacity to be in denial of what is intellectually and morally incumbent upon us to pursue.

Melville in Moby-Dick speaks of reality outracing apprehension. Apprehension in the sense not of fear or disquiet but of understanding... reality as too much for us to take in, as, for example, the white whale is too much for the Pequod and its captain. It may be that our new century is an awesomely complex white whale—scientifically in our quantumized wave particles and the manipulable stem cells of our biology, ecologically in our planetary crises of nature, technologically in our humanoid molecular computers, sexually in the rising number of our genders, intellectually in the paradoxes of our texts, and so on.

What is more natural than to rely on the saving powers of simplism? Perhaps with our dismal public conduct, so shot through with piety, we are actually engaged in a genetic engineering venture that will make a slower, dumber, more sluggish whale, one that can be harpooned and flensed, tried and boiled to light our candles. A kind of water wonderworld whale made of racism, nativism, cultural illiteracy, fundamentalist fantasy and the righteous priorities of wealth.

I summon up the year 1787, when the Constitutional Convention had done its work, and the drafted Constitution was sent out to the states for ratification. The public's excitement was palpable. Extended and vigorous statehouse debates echoed through the towns and villages, and as, one by one, the states voted to ratify, church bells rang, cheers went up from the public houses, and in the major cities the people turned out to parade with a fresh new sense of themselves as a nation. Everyone marched—tradespeople, workingmen, soldiers, women and clergy. They had floats in those days, too—most often a wagon-sized ship of state called the Union, rolling through the streets with children waving from the scuppers. Philadelphia came up with a float called the New Roof, a dome supported by thirteen pillars and ornamented with stars. It was drawn by ten white horses, and at the top was a handsome cupola surmounted by a figure of Plenty bearing her cornucopia. The ratification parades were sacramental—symbolic venerations, acts of faith. From the beginning, people saw the Constitution as a kind of sacred text for a civil society.

And with good reason: the ordaining voice of the Constitution is scriptural, but in resolutely keeping the authority for its dominion in the public consent, it presents itself as the sacred text of secular humanism.

When the ancient Hebrews broke their covenant, they suffered a loss of identity and brought disaster on themselves. Our burden, too, is covenantal. We may point to our 200-some years of national survival as an open society; we may regard ourselves as an exceptionalist, historically self-correcting nation, whose democratic values locate us just as surely as our geography—and yet we know at the same time that all through our history we have brutally excluded vast numbers of us from the shelter of the New Roof, we have broken our covenant again and again with a virtuosity verging on damnation and have been saved only by the sacrificial efforts of Constitution-revering patriots in and out of government—presidents, senators, justices, self-impoverishing lawyers, abolitionists, muckrakers, third-party candidates, suffragists, union organizers, striking workers, civil rights martyrs.

Because this President's subversion of the Constitution outdoes anything that has gone before, and as it has created large social constituencies ready to support the flag-waving ideals of an incremental fascism, we're called upon to step forward to reaffirm our covenant like these exemplars from the past.

Philosopher Richard Rorty has suggested in his book *Achieving Our Country* that the metaphysic of America's civil religion is pragmatism and its prophets are Walt Whitman and John Dewey. "The most striking feature of their redescription of our country is its thoroughgoing secularism," says Rorty. "The moral we should draw from the European past, and in particular from Christianity, is not instruction about the authority under which we should live but suggestions about how to make ourselves wonderfully different from anything that has been."

To temporize human affairs, to look not up for some applied celestial accreditation but forward, at ground level, in the endless journey to resist any authoritarian restrictions on thought or suppression of knowledge that is the public good—that is the essence of our civil religion.

It is Whitman, our great poet and pragmatic philosopher, who advises us not to be curious about God but to affix our curiosity to our own lives and the earth we live on, and then perhaps as far as we can see into the universe with our telescopes. This was the charge he gave himself, and it is the source of all the attentive love in his poetry. If we accept it as our own and decide something is right after all in a democracy that is given to a degree of free imaginative expression that few cultures in the world can tolerate, we can hope for the aroused witness, the manifold reportage, the flourishing of knowledge that will restore us to ourselves, awaken the dulled sense of our people to the public interest that is their interest, and vindicate the genius of the humanist sacred text that embraces us all. ∎

An Interview with E.L. Doctorow (2009)

E.L. Doctorow's novel, Homer and Langley *imagines the lives of New York's famous Collyer brothers, prosperous eccentrics who dropped out of society and filled their town house with collections of obsolete, strange or otherwise broken-down objects. Doctorow's narrative extends into the late twentieth century, but the real-life Collyers were found dead in 1947, Langley felled by the traps he had laid for intruders and Homer, who is blind, a victim of starvation.* —Christine Smallwood

What was your research process like?

I didn't do any research. I just used what I knew. I was a boy when they died: the whole house was discovered to be what it was, and it became instant folklore. Instant. And when my room was sloppy my mother would say, It's the Collyer brothers! I did look at photographs. I took the position that they were folklore, they were mythology, and that not research but interpretation was the proper response.

The Collyer brothers remind me a bit of the movie *Grey Gardens*.

I never made that connection. I would make a distinction—the meaning I find is quite different. I just regard those women as kind of pathetic, dysfunctional messes. But I always had a feeling that these guys, there was a secret to them. Because they'd come from a well-to-do background and opted out. That was the essential idea in my mind. Go in the house, close the door, pull down the shutters, isolate yourself from the surrounding world. It was a kind of emigration. They were leaving the country. I regarded the book as a form of breaking and entering. They lived in their imaginations.

It's also a novel about stuff.

Accounts have called them pack rats. I think that's a demeaning, inadequate phrase. What they are is aggregators. The things they bring into the house—there's a history there of the things we've thought we needed over time. At this point I think the book becomes imponderable. You can say it's about inevitable human isolation. You can say it's about entropy. You can say it's about the end of an empire. I tend to agree with any reasonable interpretation. Anyway, all of us feel we need an awful lot. And the technology keeps changing, but the minute any technology appears it becomes indispensable.

Do you have any thoughts about the Kindle or e-readers?

I don't use one. I can understand why if you're on an airplane going around the world, you'd want a Kindle. But I think books are great technology. Once they're produced they don't use any energy. If their materials are decent and sound, and you take care of them, they'll last forever. I like the feel of a book, I like to turn pages, I like to see print on paper. The pleasure of going into a bookshop, finding things you didn't even know you were looking for, discovering things—that's what we're losing now. Everyone knows in advance what they want, and they order it online or download it.

Homer and Langley seem particularly "New York."

Yes. You can see a lot of them on the street, even today. That's why it wasn't the fact that they collected things that got me going but who they were, the metaphors they created in my mind. They're people who opted out. One of my friends found a comparison with Melville's story "Bartleby, the Scrivener." That withdrawal. Yes, it's New York, but it's also American. The Beats, that was a form of withdrawal. I wrote a story years ago about a fellow, an eccentric up in Westchester County called the Leather Man. He was all dressed in animal skins and plates of leather and a big leather hat, like a Viking. He carried a staff, and he lived wandering through the woods. People would give him food. He was totally benign but shy. He lived as a wandering hermit.

Yet Homer and Langley don't travel light. What kind of opting-out is it to take the world into your home like a museum?

Making another world, pulling the world in after you. But it's a different world: a symbolic world, a doomed world. They are premature archaeologists. The novel is really anything but a psychological study of dysfunction. They're engaged in trying to create meaning for themselves and a life that makes sense to them. They have convictions. There are two images that I like from the book. One is when they're tied to the chair back-to-back in the kitchen, and Langley delivers a speech about this ideal community. The other is when they're riding a bicycle built for two down the street. The price of writing things is, you're the instant reader, and you make these discoveries—they're coming through your fingers as you're typing; you don't think of them as mental operations. Then you read what you've written, and you laugh.

What are you reading now?

I've been rereading Chekhov, some new translations of the great novellas.

What are you learning from Chekhov?

I don't know if I can learn anything from Chekhov. He's such a surpassing genius. You can figure out how a book works, break it down into its parts. But it's almost impossible with Chekhov. He splashes the words out on the page, in a seemingly artless fashion, with no particular aesthetic principle or interest in the craft. How does he write paragraphs? You don't get any sense of aesthetic organization. Time passes, people complain, nothing happens, something happens—it just sort of spreads out. Of course, there's great art in that seeming artlessness—this could happen then or five pages later; it doesn't really matter. So you can't learn from that. You just are in awe. ∎

READING JOHN LEONARD (2012)

John Leonard, who died in 2008, was literary editor of The Nation *and before that editor of the* New York Times Book Review.

John Leonard started out as a novelist but was diverted, presumably under the exigencies of making a living, his brilliance as a freelance writer being quickly recognized by editors and publishers, so that he found himself at a precocious age writing first for the *National Review*, then as a daily book reviewer for the *New York Times* and quickly as editor of the *Times Book Review*. Perhaps he recognized that his creativity was not the burrowing kind of the novelist, who lives patiently for years with a set of images and torturously realized intentions in the production of a novel. He was from the beginning a quick study, a wunderkind, writing even as a 19-year-old sophomore for the *Harvard Crimson* these already typically referential Leonardian lines in a piece he called "The Cambridge Scene": "Did not Eliot return to dead cultures, ancient languages, and the Legend of the Fisher King? Did not Yeats sustain himself on the Irish folklore? Did not Lawrence traipse across continents to Mexico, seeking the meaning of the Aztecs, the wisdom of primitive man?... Yours is a motel civilization.... Your art makes no sense and your music is too loud."

No wonder he abandoned Harvard for the University of California, Berkeley. But in the cold war fifties, he was to touch down in New York, and his youthful longing for whatever came before, whether the authenticity of folklore or the romantic radicalism of *fin de siècle* Greenwich Village ("There used to be a time when John Reed and Lincoln Steffens lived at the same Village address.... No more.... The Village today is populated by the smug, the self-conscious, and the literary sycophants"), was, in a sense, the young man's common enough generalized anxiety of influence—his fear that he and his era could never match the grand human proportions of what had been previously conceived. Or was it what he imagined had been conceived—his idealistic sense of a human greatness that he could never attribute to what he found in the world around him? He would all his life be an avowed skeptic but with a religious sensibility that would make of him a celebrant of the moments when he did glimpse something of the full expression of human capacity. And perhaps, in a kind of quest, he was to wade right in, immersing himself totally in what imaginative work his life and times had to offer, his idealism reconfigured as a very sharp, keen wit that could with authority assess books and ideas for what they are.

If you consider a collection of John Leonard's essays and reviews as a lifelong accounting, you will have a good idea of what went on of significance in the latter half of the American twentieth century and the first years of the twenty-first. Though reviewing literary work was his calling, it did not box him in. He was a born freelancer, going wherever that tenuous life led him, from the monuments of high culture that he was inspired to celebrate, to the commodities of the low, from which he would take gleanings where most of us would find none. It is difficult to understand how, with his immense reading and the sustenance his mind sought, he could have sat himself down year after year to examine the products of television. Yet there he was, considering what it meant when sitcom settings moved from the kitchen to the living room, and the family characters sitting on the living room couch, and presumably watching their television, seemed to be watching him. Or there he was, considering what these programs said about fatherhood and motherhood in America. He understood the presumptive sociology in the arrays of sitcoms and to what degree they reflected American domestic reality or in fact helped to shape it.

But the novel was to Leonard the presiding art—always in its intentions, if only occasionally in its realization, a major act of the culture. He says in the piece "Reading for My Life" that "popular culture is where we go to talk to and agree with one another; to simplify ourselves; to find our herd.... Whereas books are where we go alone to complicate ourselves." He is an excited first responder when the work is García Márquez's *One Hundred Years of Solitude*. "You emerge from this marvelous novel as if from a dream, the mind on fire.... So richly realized are the Buendías that they invite comparison with the Karamazovs and Sartorises." One book reminding him of another is a Leonardian characteristic, as if books are antiphonal calls and responses. It is in his most exultant reviews that his words tumble forth in catalogs of ascription, as he tries to convey as much of the book as he can short of quoting the thing in its entirety: "Family chronicle, then, and political tour de force, and metaphysical romp, and, intentionally, a cathedral of words, perceptions, and details," he says of the García Márquez, amounting to "the declaration of a state of mind: solitude being one's admission of one's own mortality and one's discovery that the terrible apprehension is itself mortal, dies with you, must be rediscovered and forgotten again, endlessly."

The great English critic Frank Kermode said that every piece of literary criticism rewrites the text it examines. Less dogmatically expressed, the idea is that a work is not completed until the reader animates the text, as if the lines of a novel are a printed circuit through which the force of the reader's life will flow. And so not just the critic but every reader rewrites the text, and the rewrite is a measure of the reader's mind. Leonard, with his mind of swiftly moving, synaptically fired thoughts, so that his sentences seem to race along and sometimes pile up in their effort to stay abreast, will usually find the expanded possibilities of a text. But it is not only his capacious mind that distinguishes him; it is the wisdom of his critical decency. When he attends to someone's work, there is not only illumination but a beneficence of spirit, as if, even when he doesn't like something and will tell us why, he is still at work championing the literary project.

Of course, some writers did arouse his sporting nature—Norman Mailer for one, a writer for whom he had a considerable, if not blind, regard and whose novel *Harlot's*

Ghost is examined in the closest thing to a forensic review you ever will read. On another occasion Leonard reviewed a late Mailer work, *The Spooky Art: Some Thoughts on Writing*, taking it down quietly, gently, and in parentheses.

Mailer: That is one of the better tests of the acumen of the writer. How subtle, how full of nuance, how original, is his or her sense of the sinister?

Leonard: (George Eliot? Chekhov? Stendhal?)

Mailer: Few good writers come out of prison. Incarceration, I think, can destroy a man's ability to write.

Leonard: (Cervantes, Dostoevsky, Rimbaud, Koestler, Genet, Havel, Solzhenitsyn?)

Mailer: It is not only that no other man writes so well about women [as D.H. Lawrence], but indeed is there a woman who can?

Leonard: (If not Doris Lessing, Nadine Gordimer, Grace Paley, Toni Morrison, or Colette, how about Shikibu Murasaki?)

For Leonard could be very funny, his prose skimming along with a breeziness, every page filled with wordplay—cross-cultural allusions, puns, overreaching metaphors, phrases stolen from German metaphysics, lines from movies, double entendres, political riffs, as if to persuade us that, as serious as the critical enterprise might be, we are not to worry, no solemn self-importance is to be found here, that he is of the street, that if he'd been back in Elizabethan times, watching a Shakespeare play at the Globe, he'd be standing in the pit.

Leonard was a political animal, and he waded into the social and cultural battles of the day, always pleased to have a forum but never mincing his words by way of holding on to it. He was not kind to the media—*People*, *Newsweek*, the *Wall Street Journal*, *Cosmopolitan*—for their buffoon-like coverage of the AIDS epidemic, the racism implicit in their reporting, the prissy misinformation they spread. Speaking of the Iranian fatwa, or contract, out for Salman Rushdie, author of *The Satanic Verses*, he scorns the book chains that won't sell the book, the Catholic and Jewish religious figures who deplore its publication and those of Rushdie's fellow writers who demand that it be pulped. Of Richard Nixon's memoir, *Six Crises*, he says, "Nixon has nothing to offer this nation but the cheap sort of second-rate sainthood he is here busy trying to manufacture." And he functions as a droll chorus to Bob Dylan's tactically cunning ascent to musical stardom in the 1960s, titling his review of books about the singer "Blowing His Nose in the Wind."

Finally what we realize from the intense life in his prose is that Leonard held back nothing, neither hiding behind a formal diction nor modulating the demeanor he carried to every piece in deference to the publication running it. In the realm of cultural journalism there was no one quite like him.

He gave everything he was, each time out. To read his work today is to encounter a mind still thinking, a voice still alive.

There was something religious about John Leonard, however much of a principled skeptic he may have been. With his pale complexion, his round eyeglasses, there was a translucence to him such as is given to the spiritually employed. It was as if he had been assigned, somewhere off the earth, to take note of writers and to testify to their value, and was, willy-nilly, a patron saint of the writing trade, of the storymakers, of the Grub Street international bunch of us. With his love of language and his faith in its relevance to human salvation, our own inadvertent, secular humanist patron saint.

■

Home
(2015)

1.

There has always been another world. In Neolithic times, they built megaliths, steles, timed to the solstices—so they had some astronomical sense. Failing that, there was always a sabertoothed tiger to run them down. In the Grecian Bronze Age was invented the cast of maniac characters known as the gods—each with a different competitive function usually attached to features of the natural world, but showing clearly an awareness of something in existence other than humankind. The pre-Socratics scientized this and spoke of elemental forces that powered the world, and they argued as to which were more elemental than others—water, fire, air or earth. Then came Democritus with his astonishing theory of the invisible atom as the basis of everything. Plato allegorized the problem, describing a cave of firelit shadows where most men lived, unaware of the sun outside. All of this was, of course, monotheisticized by the Abrahamic religions—one supreme Reality with His own reasons, His dos and don'ts. And in the eighteenth century, Immanuel Kant spoke of "things in themselves" as being beyond our phenomenological knowing—that the world was something else than what we could actually know, captured as we were in our own minds.

John Searle is a contemporary philosopher with an unalterable belief in "things in themselves." That makes him, philosophically, a Realist. Reality, in his refreshing advanced diction, is composed of "brute facts," which for Searle consist entirely "of physical particles in fields of force, and in which some of these particles are organized into systems that are conscious biological beasts, such as ourselves." The examples he cites of such ur-Reality are "mountains, planets, H_2O molecules, rivers, crystals, and babies." I would include the climatic biomes. But the examples of Reality are endless, of course, and include the stars in the skies, the skies and, in fact, what we understand as the entire universe. So Searle finds it convenient to wrap up Reality by reference to "the atomic theory of matter" and "natural selection." These, he says, are the constituent facts of "a world independent of our representations of it."

What we are left with is the world of our own devising, to which Searle gives the traditional term "social reality." Social reality is institutional, a matter of our historical invention. "Money, property, marriage, governments, elections, football games, cocktail parties" are Searle's deftly chosen examples of social reality. They are factual, but they require "human institutions for their existence." By way of alerting those keenly assured of the leftist subtexts of all philosophic thought, however conservative, I would add as examples of social reality the National Rifle Association, oil and coal companies, and *Citizens United v. Federal Election Commission*.

The work of Searle's from which I've quoted is *The Construction of Social Reality* (the Free Press edition, copyright ©1995 by Searle). We need not follow the intricacies of his discussion of social reality, whose metaphysics fascinate him—how, he asks, do we get from atomic particles to this?—nor linger with his insistent defense of Realism. I give him all that and take his two realities for my own purposes.

2.

To speak of the construction of social reality is to affirm the remarkable history of our species, which, as we tell our children, invented the wheel, made fire, discovered farming, built ships to sail the seas, and invented railroads, horseless carriages, aircraft, instant communication over great distances—all in an endless story of human progress through millions of years, advancing in its modes of social organization from tribes to nation states, from kings and despots to parliaments, from designated slaves to free people living now in vast, electrically powered and digitized cities with hospitals, libraries, museums and theaters, with poets of many languages, saloons, stock markets, churches, universities, zoos, national treasuries, and streets filled with the literate and well clothed. (If murderous war has been a constant, no one would think to claim for us angelicism.)

And within this historic world, the real world of the "brute facts," genetically manipulated or penetrated with particle accelerators, seems to be surprisingly unresisting, subject to such resourceful pumping of its oil, mining of its minerals, stripping of its forests, and fishing of its seas as to amount to a Reality that is no match for the social realities we've constructed from it.

Joseph Conrad, in his novel *Lord Jim*, says of a minor character that he could not survive except within a well-developed civilization. No author sneers at his own characters as royally as Conrad, but in fact that dependence describes most of us. And why not, since civilizations are what the species has been designing for itself in its great epochal struggles to endure. In a favorable light, human history may be seen as the colossally effective enterprise of converting some of the brute facts of Reality into realities on which we can survive. Until now, as a geologically clocked obsessiveness, it has been, with the expansive genius of *Homo sapiens*, an immeasurable mythic wresting of life from its inhospitality. And the vast unknowable world we inhabit would seem to be represented in our imaginations only by the occasional mountain lion overturning a garbage can in the suburbs.

3.

Yet we have learned, with the knowledge that has made human beings conquistadors of the earth, that such executive success for so long brings with it—what to call it?—a cosmological arrogance. That arrogance, most compactly described, is the anthropic principle. It states that the exploding universe was formed fortuitously of such a specific chemical stew as to make the appearance of human life on the earth inevitable. Never mind the billions of years of gaseous storms, the firing up of photons and the slow whirling of constellations—according to the anthropic principle, it looks suspiciously as if we are the point of it all. And so, despite its hypothetical tone—there is said to be both a weak and a strong principle—we can hear in it a quasi-religious self-congratulation, another reading perhaps of Genesis, wherein the culmination of God's great work comes on the sixth day with the supreme creation of the Bible writers themselves.

4.

If there is a consensus among scientists that the Reality independent of our representations of it is changing its nature, there is everywhere a resistance to the idea. To someone living in a great city, where the natural world is represented by a park with benches, life is made from the sum of social realities. If you go to work in an office building and are occupied with the pressures of the job, the competitive business institution, your mind is so busy and the circumstances of survival so personal that there is no time for the thought of a vengeful Reality. Or if you are the single parent providing your children with their breakfast cereal. Or if you are at war, lying in the sand with your rifle at the ready, these climatic circumstances demand of you a vocabulary too exotic to be seriously part of the thinking of someone inured to a private, if not to a powerless, life.

To others, the so-called crisis of climate change is no more than the usual daily business of the planet—icebergs calving, songbirds going silent, obscure species of frogs dying in their ponds. Those who calmly hold to this view choose to believe nothing at all is happening that is inconsistent with normal changes in biological diversification—the thriving of some creatures, the dying out of others—or, regarding variations in the weather, what we have always known to be the hurricane season on this continent, the monsoons over there. Though, of course, they choose not to know of the climatic biomes, or to believe that climate and weather are two entirely different things. People have settled the earth where the climate made farming possible, or because desert sands were livable, or because prevalent tropical temperatures made life easy. The habitation of the earth, and growth of cultures, reflect age-old patterns of human distribution. This—the prevalence of sustaining lifelong climatic regions, not frogs in a pond—is what is changing.

And then there are those who not only reject the idea of a global climate crisis but do so with scorn or suspicion, finding in the scientific consensus nothing less than a conspiracy. Though why a scientific conspiracy should exist, or to what purpose, is never made clear. But it is politicians, officeholders of the right, who broadcast this paranoia.

Finally, there are the corporate leaders in the energy industries—the coal operators, the oil producers—who would prevent any regulation of carbon emissions or other modifications of their business practices. As the presumptive beneficiaries of the human colonization of Earth, they are afflicted with the latent conceit of triumphalism, in which social reality is Reality, the two are merged, and there is no distinguishing them.

5.

But there is a dynamic here that is nothing new. When Galileo reported his telescopically informed conclusion that Copernicus was right—it was the earth that moved around the sun—he was tried for heresy by the Inquisition. He recanted, though he did not entirely avert punishment, spending the rest of his life under house arrest. He had discovered a brute fact that contradicted the prevalent social reality of church teaching, that the sun moved around the earth—social realties being even to this day as much a matter of the political manipulation of fantasy as of inventions such as the cellphone. It was only in 1992 that the Catholic Church admitted that Galileo might be right. While we no longer accuse scientists of heresy, there is a residual suspicion of the subversive capacity of science, with its famous "method," to overturn the comfortable social realities that people find to their advantage. The high clergy of the Middle Ages were beneficiaries of the religious domination of society: they ate quite well and dressed in finery. It seems apparent that today, too, those who abjure the ineluctable Reality of global warming are the conservatives among us, the same Republicans who themselves live quite well and do not like universal healthcare, or raises in the minimum wage, or any government oversight of investment banks. If they are not all malefactors of great wealth, they tend to include those of the corporate executive culture who can't abide any interest, even humankind's, that is not in their corporation's interest. And if the class of citizen-deniers includes Tea Party exegetes not themselves in the economic upper percentiles, we can't condemn them, so pathetically misinformed are they in the face of a looming planetary crisis.

It is true that people in other countries want what we have, and so they cut down trees, and poach, and cook with coal fire, in that great quest for "me" that is the mark of our species. But I speak of the American situation. There is a preoccupation here with "Holy Scripture" that is dogged, hates Darwin, and insists on the literal and sacred truth of primitive documents thousands of years old. About this, nothing can be done.

6.

But someone must bear the responsibility for this widespread national resistance, someone with propagandistic resources, someone richer than most and so in a position to negate, deny, and hold up to scorn any reasonable scientific explanation of what is happening to our planet.

In this country, we cede to the plutocrats. I would choose the Koch brothers as likely villains, those malefactors of great wealth, except that their malefaction is only incidental to the problem. Their sin, as influential men of wealth hiding their own brutal interests behind a libertarian facade, is worse than that.

Look at it this way: as Americans, we pride ourselves on getting things done, as people knowing what to do and when to do it—this is as basic an American identity as there is. From Ben Franklin on up through the Franklin Roosevelt of the Second World War, we have been archetypally more than given to solve any task, secure any dream. Therefore, the Koch brothers' failure is only incidental to their wealth. Theirs is the sin of what can hardly be imagined as a factor of power: it is maladaptive failure, the failure to understand the realities and do something about them. The Kochs have lost that; they are staggering about in the woods with no idea what to do beyond preserving their fiefdom. We need not go into the reasons for this failure—psychological, emotional, structural—the cost to us is too great.

7.

At this stage of the climatic problem, it is not the priests, rabbis or ministers among us who are saying that "pride goeth before the Fall"; it is the scientists. That interests me—this turn to religious moralizing on the part of the secular community. It may represent an enormous cultural shift, a kind of re-establishment of a new liturgical authority. Because it is an undeniable worship of the earth that would ask us to save it. If anyone were to walk the streets with a sign saying THE END IS NEAR, I would expect it to be someone with a PhD in physics. This would explain the public aversion of some to the idea of science: that its practitioners speak, however technically, as prophets—a prophet, of course, being someone to be ignored.

It may be with some resentment that we feel, after all that has been done to the earth in many thousands of years, that it should fall to us, to our generations, to pay the price. Yet it was only the Industrial Revolution of the eighteenth century that sped us into recognizably modern times. Wordsworth wrote in the early 1800s: "The world is too much with us; late and soon, / Getting and spending, we lay waste our powers: / Little we see in Nature that is ours...."

For those who do imagine a catastrophe of astronomical magnitude, our imagination is limited. What do movies know? We may see cities in smoking ruins. With winds which we have never known for their iciness, and waters for their heaving, thunderous rages, and morning suns burning our lands to cinders, and all of it happening consistent with each of our maniacally trashed biomes. Perhaps then we will see wars for potable water, tillable land. And who will be left after the plagues but some lonely stragglers looking for community—and finding no other humans but hideous creatures of natural selection who have sprouted energetically in this new, unrecognizable Reality.

But there is no telling what will be. The planet going through its agonies may end up quietly enough—just not the home we thought it was. It is a few seers in our time who remind us that, for all our intrepid world-making social realities, we are dealing with something inexplicable: Reality is still there, as mysterious as ever. Einstein tells us that scientific knowledge is like a searchlight whose expanding beam brings more and more of what was once dark into the light—but as it does, so does the circumference of darkness expand. ∎

AFTERWORD

Victor Navasky

E.L. Doctorow, who died on July 21 at the age of 84, was not only a personal pal; he was a supporter of, investor in, and contributor to this magazine and, as the world knows, a gifted, original, and über-relevant novelist.

I first met Edgar in the late 1960s, when he was editor in chief of Dial Press, where his authors included James Baldwin and Norman Mailer. At the time, I was editing and publishing *Monocle*, a small journal of political satire.

We had an idea for a book that became *Report From Iron Mountain: On the Possibility and Desirability of Peace*. Its premise was that the US government had commissioned a special study group to plan the transition from a war economy to a peace economy—but the group, which met in secret, found that without war or the threat of it, the economy would collapse, so it quashed the report. The book was written by Leonard Lewin, with input from economist John Kenneth Galbraith, *Monocle* editors Marvin Kitman and Richard Lingeman (later executive editor of *The Nation*), and yours truly.

Although all of its footnotes were to real sources, the report itself was, of course, a hoax. But we wanted a publisher who would list it as nonfiction and not let the sales force know otherwise. In Edgar Doctorow, along with Dial Press publisher Richard Baron, we found the perfect co-conspirators. When a reporter from the *New York Times* called to ask whether it was a real, government-commissioned study, Doctorow advised him: If you don't believe it, check out the footnotes. And when the reporter called the Johnson White House, the officials—not knowing whether or not the Kennedy administration had commissioned it—simply responded, "No comment." The *Times* ran a front-page story saying this was possibly a hoax and possibly a secret government document, and the book ended up on the *Times* bestseller list!

Little did we know that this episode, exploiting the complicated line between fact and fiction, was to prefigure Doctorow's remarkable career as he went on to write, among other works raising critical historical, political, and cultural questions, *The Book of Daniel* (inspired by the case of Julius and Ethel Rosenberg), *Ragtime*, *Billy Bathgate*, and *The March*.

All of this is a matter of public record. What is not generally known, however, is Edgar's unique contribution to this magazine. I am not only talking about the 22 extraordinary articles, essays, meditations, and speeches by him that we were privileged to publish, commencing in 1978, but we can start there. They ranged from his thoughts on "The Rise of Ronald Reagan," and why it was wrong for the writers group PEN (on whose board he sat) to invite Secretary of State George Shultz to address its annual gathering, to his meditations "The State of Mind of the Union" (1986) and "A Citizen Reads the Constitution" (1987), not to mention his subversive reflections on "Why We Are Infidels" (2003).

Were it not for Edgar, I might never have had the opportunity to edit *The Nation* in the first place. Long story short: When it became known in 1977 that James Storrow, the publisher and owner of the magazine, was ready to pass the baton to the next generation, young Hamilton Fish and I were one of 20-odd parties that expressed interest. I was a candidate to become editor, while Ham (whom I had gotten to know during Ramsey Clark's 1974 campaign to succeed

Jacob Javits as New York senator) set out to raise funds to buy the money-losing magazine and sustain it while we did our best to raise it to a position of self-sustainability. It was Edgar who, fresh from his *Ragtime* triumph and without being asked, wrote a check for $10,000 so that Ham would have some "walking-around money" (as Edgar called it) while he did his best to raise the $1 million that would make the deal possible.

And when Storrow balked at signing the needed option agreement, it was Edgar, along with Ralph Nader and a couple of other longtime *Nation* enthusiasts, who attended a key meeting that helped persuade Storrow—who, it turned out, was not quite psychologically ready to yield control—to sign the deal that enabled fundraising to go forward. Some years later, Doctorow, who had been at Kenyon College with Paul Newman (Edgar liked to joke that it wasn't until the actor graduated that he started to get the good parts), set up a dinner date for me with Paul and his wife, Joanne Woodward. The result: Newman became the magazine's single largest outside annual financial supporter until his death.

Edgar was always modest when responding to questions about where he got the ideas for his books, almost as if he had nothing to do with it. As Edgar tells it, he was sitting at his desk, having written 150 pages about a couple much like the Rosenbergs from the vantage of an omniscient narrator, when suddenly a voice (which turned out to be that of their son) emerged from his typewriter, and out came *The Book of Daniel*. Or he was on his porch in New Rochelle, when what should come riding down the road but the idea for *Ragtime*, with Coalhouse Walker at the wheel.

Where did Edgar get the idea for *Loon Lake*? He was driving in the Adirondacks, saw a sign that said LOON LAKE, and that was it. "You've got to let things happen to you to write," he said. A friend once said that Edgar—a student of John Crowe Ransom, the Kenyon College professor considered to be the founder of the New Criticism—was "a walking refutation of the intentional fallacy." When I asked him what would have happened if he'd passed a sign for Lake Placid instead, Edgar replied, "I did pass the sign, but I didn't notice it." Then again, he once told an interviewer: "The fact of the matter is that for the fiction writer, once the book is composed, the fictive machinery keeps going—it doesn't turn off. Whatever you used to write the book, you're now using your memory to create a fiction about it."

We will miss you, Edgar, with your arched right eyebrow that let us know your unique appreciation for the interaction of fiction and nonfiction, the comic and the serious, and how you transcended the simplistic distinctions between high and low culture.

The first time Edgar invited Annie (the woman who was to become Mrs. Navasky) and me to the Doctorow home in New Rochelle, he and his brother Donald gave a recital on banjo and guitar. On another occasion, before a *Nation* Town Hall event in support of Poland's Solidarity movement, Edgar invited Pete Seeger over to learn the Solidarity protest songs in Polish from a visiting member of the movement, so that he might introduce them at Town Hall. If words could sing, this note would end with Pete singing Woody Guthrie's "So Long, It's Been Good to Know Yuh."

∎